CONVERSATIONAL CAPITAL

CONVERSATIONAL CAPITAL

HOW TO CREATE STUFF
PEOPLE LOVE TO TALK ABOUT

BY

BERTRAND CESVET
WITH TONY BABINSKI & ERIC ALPER

A
SID LEE
PROJECT

Vice President, Publisher: Tim Moore
Associate Publisher and Director of Marketing: Amy Neidlinger
Operations Manager: Gina Kanouse
Development Editor: Russ Hall
Digital Marketing Manager: Julie Phifer
Marketing Coordinator: Megan Colvin
Cover and Interior Designer: SID LEE
Managing Editor: Kristy Hart
Senior Project Editor: Lori Lyons
Copy Editor: Deadline Driven Publishing
Proofreader: Water Crest Publishing, Inc.
Indexer: WordWise Publishing Services
Senior Compositor: Jake McFarland
Manufacturing Buyer: Dan Uhrig

FT Press offers excellent discounts on this book when ordered in quantity for bulk purchases or special sales. For more information, please contact U.S. Corporate and Government Sales, 1-800-382-3419, corpsales@pearsontechgroup.com. For sales outside the U.S., please contact International Sales at international@pearson.com.

Pearson Education LTD.
Pearson Education Australia PTY, Limited.
Pearson Education Singapore, Pte. Ltd.
Pearson Education North Asia, Ltd.
Pearson Education Canada, Ltd.
Pearson Educatión de Mexico, S.A. de C.V.
Pearson Education—Japan
Pearson Education Malaysia, Pte. Ltd.

Library of Congress Cataloging-in-Publication Data
Cesvet, Bertrand, 1964-
  How to create stuff people will love to talk about / Bertrand Cesvet, Tony Babindki, Eric Alper.
    p. cm.
  Includes index.
  ISBN 0-13-714550-0 (hbk. : alk. paper) 1. Branding (Marketing) I. Babindki, Tony, 1964- II. Alper, Eric, 1985- III. Title.
  HF5415.1255.C47 2009
  658.8'27--dc22
                          2008013639

To my wife Josée Noiseux and our children Gabrielle and Emma,
my greatest supporters, my inspiration, and the loves of my life.

BC

To my parents Tom and Maria Babinski, and as always,
to my wife Julie Kavcic and our children Sophie, Max, and Lily.

TB

To my loving parents for their undying support
and encouragement.

EA

TABLE OF CONTENTS

ACKNOWLEDGMENTS

This book is the product of numerous conversations with several inspiring friends, clients, and colleagues. In addition to my two fabulous co-authors Tony Babinski and Eric Alper, who have been extremely stimulating and competent partners, I would like to thank a few other important people.

Firstly, I would like to thank my business partner, François Lacoursière, for his formidable intellect and intensity. This book would not have happened without our memorable walks and epic conversations along Lake Léman and the streets of London. Similarly, I would like to thank my wife, Josée Noiseux, for all her patience and, more importantly, her very valuable insight into the development of the Conversational Capital idea.

Secondly, I would like to thank my other SID LEE partners: Jean-François Bouchard, Philippe Meunier, Martin Gauthier, Daniel Fortier, Pétula Bouchard, Kristian Manchester, Eva Van Den Bulcke, Karim Kendjouh, Louis-Thomas Pelletier, Harm Sas, Niels van de Walle, Hélène Godin, Jean-François Fortin, George Giampuranis, and Vito Piazza, for believing in me and for investing in my ideas.

Thirdly, I would like to thank all the SID LEE employees with whom I have had the great pleasure of experimenting and implementing the concept of Conversational Capital: Francis Béland, Sakchin Bessette, Stéphane Bernier, Jean-François

Bouchard (at Cirque du Soleil), Lukas Derksen, Andrea Doyon, Michel Dubuc, Emily Fowler, Jean-Julien Guyot, June Leong Son, Raphaëlle Levy, Alex Pasini, Connie Ponari, and Gabrielle St-Pierre.

Also, I would like to thank all the clients and friends who have also been instrumental in developing this book: Luc Arbour, Alain Auclair, Daniel Audet, Jim Bailey, Carlo Bianchini, Kai and Frank Binder, Bertrand Charest, Mario D'Amico, Hermann Deininger, Rupert Duchesne, Christian Eckart, Joanne Fillion, Mitchell Garber, David Giguère, Jean Goulet, Jim Herler, Pierre Ladouceur, Guy Laliberté, Daniel Lamarre, Ted Mager, Ben Pruess, Tom Ramsden, David Van Kalsbeek, and Nicole Vollerbregt.

Finally, I would like to thank the very talented people who are responsible for the production and the promotion of this book: Jessica Barboza, Marie-Hélène Benoît, Ziggy Hagopian, Russ Hall, Sjoerd Koopman, Marie-Josée Lamy, and Cindy Levac. Last, but not the least, thanks to the entire FT Press team, in particular Tim Moore, Ami Neidlinger, Lori Lyons, and Jake McFarland.

Thank you for believing in me and in SID LEE.

BC, Montréal, March 2008

ABOUT THE AUTHORS

Bertrand Cesvet is chairman and chief strategist of SID LEE, a leading provider of experiential design and creative services, with offices in Montréal and Amsterdam. He provides creative and strategic leadership on marketing communications and experience design projects for clients such as adidas, Red Bull, Cirque du Soleil, and MGM Mirage. He lives in Montréal with his wife Josée and daughters Gabrielle and Emma.

Tony Babinski is a Montréal-based writer, creative director, and filmmaker. He has worked with SID LEE since 2000 and is the author of *Cirque du Soleil: 20 Years Under the Sun*, the authorized history of Cirque du Soleil. He lives in Montréal with his wife Julie and children Sophie, Max, and Lily.

Eric Alper is a strategist for SID LEE. He has kept a blog about Conversational Capital going since 2006. He has also developed and written the Conversational Capital blog.

HOW THIS BOOK CAME TOGETHER

This book is the result of a series of conversations.

Conversational Capital was born when Bertrand Cesvet was on a walk around Lake Léman in Switzerland with Fran-çois Lacoursiére, a long-time partner at SID LEE. Taking in the beauty of the Alps around them, they told themselves that *this* would be an experience they would be sure to tell their friends and family about. Ever the creative strategists, they instinctively turned that thought into a question, "Why?" Why would they talk about this destination more than any other? Why would they one day share stories about this alpine walk, and not, say, a lunch stop in Sarnia, Ontario? Indeed, why is anyone inclined to talk more about one experience than another?

That nagging question led them to examine what aspects of certain experiences trigger positive word-of-mouth. The results discussed and developed with François and others at SID LEE were collected in a 2005 white paper. The white paper was then posted at conversationalcapital.com, a blog that Bertrand asked Eric Alper to keep to test the insights and develop them further.

Our observations about Conversational Capital soon began to become more detailed and refined. Bertrand approached Tony Babinski about working together with Eric on this book in the fall of 2006.

The result is a true collaboration. We have thrown ideas around, engaged in vigorous debate, and helped each other clarify our thoughts and observations. Throughout the process, members of the SID LEE team have shared their views as well, in particular François Lacoursiére, Alex Pasini, Jean-François Bouchard, and Sjoerd Koopman.

It must be said, and not for the first time that Conversational Capital is not a system. It is a collection of insights and observations about how positive word-of-mouth is generated and how that change turns marketing on its head. It is an ongoing exploration and a theory in constant evolution. Challenging and refining those insights and observations is a work in progress, and one that we hope will include readers like you. Throughout this book, we offer opportunities for you to question and respond to what we've written. We invite you to send your feedback to conversationalcapital.com, where we hope to keep the conversation going. In the end, your contribution will help to make Conversational Capital a more true reflection of our business's best practices.

THIS IS AN OPEN-SOURCE BOOK

My name is Sjoerd Koopman, and I did not write this book! I wish I had. In many ways, the insights in this book reflect the way I look at and connect with the world around me. Simply put, it has fine-tuned the way I relate to consumer experiences. I've taken it to heart, and I expect it will have the same effect on you.

I've found that I just can't put this book away on the shelf after reading it. The book has gotten under my skin. Perhaps this is because it raises more questions than it answers. The authors intended this. *Conversational Capital* isn't meant to simply explain. It's an invitation to explore, question, and exchange opinions.

Conversational Capital is itself the initiation of a conversation. The authors have included questions and answers at the end of the chapters. These are not meant to be definitive—they are intended to stimulate further questions and discussion. That exchange continues at www.conversationalcapital.com. The website is an open invitation to take part in the process of defining what is out there that truly has the power to make our relationships and experiences richer.

As the managing director of SID LEE's intellectual capital effort, my role is to ensure www.conversationalcapital.com becomes a freewheeling, open-source destination for more content relevant to Conversational Capital. I encourage you to join me in challenging and cajoling the authors of this book and in contributing your own knowledge, media, and opinions to what will become the shared work of a tribe.

If, like me, you wish you had written this book, there's hope for us all. This may be the first publication about Conversational Capital, but we hope it won't be the last. Through the website, we hope to gather a multitude of voices whose echoes will be heard in our ongoing exploration.

To many decision makers, the message of Conversational Capital may appear frightening and uncontrollable; however, after going through it, I expect most will recognize how inherently logical it is. This book is not about a safe route to success. It is about understanding how we create stuff people will love to talk about it. In that creation process, you should find yourself challenged enough to be a little afraid; if not, you haven't gone far enough.

CONVERSATIONAL CAPITAL IS MOBILE

GET THE LATEST CONVERSATIONAL CAPITAL INTERVIEWS, RECOMMENDATIONS AND NEWS IN VIDEO, AUDIO AND TEXT ON YOUR MOBILE.

MOBILE CAMERA PHONE* USERS:

1. Point your mobile to http://conversationalcapital.com/mobile.

2. Select and download a reader.

3. Open the reader on your phone.

4. Take a snapshot of icon to the left, follow the instructions, and voilà.

ALL OF THIS CONTENT ALSO CAN BE FOUND AT
HTTP://CONVERSATIONALCAPITAL.COM/QR

*NOTE: NOT ALL PHONES ARE COMPATIBLE, BUT MORE ARE BEING ENABLED DAILY. MOBILE CARRIER BANDWIDTH FEES MAY APPLY.

Sjoerd Koopman
Managing Director Intellectual Capital, SID LEE
Skoopman@sidlee.com

FOREWORD BY HERMANN DEININGER

What makes an individual move from a mere consumer of products to a loyal customer or even a brand ambassador? As contemporary marketers, our goal is to secure advocates who present our brand for us.

In this day and age, people don't care about brands by virtue of the fact that they're merely satisfying. Indeed, in a market with healthy competition and high expectations, brands must look at what they offer far beyond the product itself. People care because some, better than others, create an intense, enduring and meaningful sense of connection and emotion that shapes their own identity. This phenomenon, very much evident in fashion, is driven by a deceivingly simple quality: meaning. This is the added value that can be crafted and subsequently leveraged to endear, convert, or compel the individual to embrace one brand over another with more than just a passing whim. Brands colour our characters, our stories, our values, and at their very essence, our identities, which is why smart brands give people something to colour with.

The identity-shaping power of brands is amplified by intensity—a sense of dynamism, discovery and, importantly for our work at adidas, integrity that reinforces deep meaning. Intense brands are those that create experiences that connect with people; that reach, touch, and engage the values and attitudes of a particular audience. Layering intensity on top of meaning results in cascading word-of-mouth.

At adidas, we are fortunate to be able to draw upon a wealth of diverse and rich artifacts—both past and present. Our story, from our heritage and commitment to sport, to our iconic sense of style and connection to global pop culture is rooted in a humble and open sense of inclusiveness which fosters new connections to people daily. The lesson implicit in this book is how to make this happen; how to make stuff [and experiences] people love to talk about.

Rather than presenting a how-to on exploiting word-of-mouth, the authors of *Conversational Capital* empower you with the tools to engineer conversations, from the ground up. They lay out a clear path to creating powerful, relevant brands that get talked about.

Conversational Capital is a challenge to marketers everywhere to engage consumers and play a meaningful role in their lives. It marks a fundamental schism in the marketing world between brands that scream from the rooftops and those that create a meaningful, intense, and sustained connection with global citizens. This call to arms is universally relevant, whether you sell commodified widgets or craft shoes for bobsledders.

Hermann Deininger
Chief Marketing Officer
Sport Style
adidas AG

INTRODUCTION

This is a book about why certain brands outperform the competition. Through close observation, we've determined how market leaders inject intensity into their products and services and turn them into experiences that truly matter to consumers. This is the "stuff" we refer to on the cover of this book. These highly charged experiences provide incendiary fuel for conversations that consumers engage in to define who they are. Because they have so much identity defining and affirming significance, having the power to shape such experiences is the new Holy Grail for businesses bent on leadership. And, like the Holy Grail, it is ultimately mysterious and elusive.

Or is it? We've written this book because we believe that creating such experiences is a process you can influence. It's not as mysterious as you may think. It is something you can manage through observation, insight, and, most importantly, creativity.

Our belief isn't just a matter of opinion. It's rooted in our direct experience with one of the biggest conversation-generating successes of the last quarter century: Cirque du Soleil.

In 2001, Cirque du Soleil asked us to redesign its website. The company was already an international live entertainment giant. With eight ground-breaking shows running in various traveling and permanent installations around the world, Cirque had achieved gross annual revenues of over 500 million dollars a year and counting. At the time, before user-generated content began maximizing the Internet's potential to create thriving online communities, Cirque already had a fan club boasting 300,000 dedicated members.

We soon became Cirque's main marketing communications agency and have been with the company ever since. Cirque du Soleil now has five permanent shows in Las Vegas, one in Orlando, one in Macao, and nine shows on tour. They have expanded into television, film, music, and, more recently, lifestyle products and experiences. Their business keeps growing—and perhaps the most amazing thing about the company's remarkable evolution into a cultural icon is that *it took place with almost no mass marketing to support it.*

Before we began working on the new site, we had to come to terms with just how much the Cirque du Soleil brand meant to its fans. Almost everyone who had ever seen a Cirque show liked it. Many of them *loved* it and became repeat fans. Perhaps more importantly, a significant number of Cirque fans described the shows as *life-changing* experiences and became brand ambassadors, carrying the Cirque torch with them wherever they went.

All of this happened without even a nod of recognition to how things are supposed to work in conventional marketing practice. For decades, the accepted wisdom in industry circles has been that brands succeed only if a ton of money is thrown in the direction of mass marketing. Want to be noticed? Spend big on media. Make sure that television and print ads with a simple, easy-to-understand message about your brand get out there in front of as many people as possible, over and over and over again. Combining maximum reach with maximum frequency is the only way to go.

Except that didn't happen with Cirque du Soleil. Instead, the company's success grew organically, through *word-of-mouth*. Cirque is a success because people have taken it to heart, and made it part of their own personal narratives—something they not only talk about with others, but that also defines who they are.

Nothing is more powerful than when consumers make your story part of their story. This is especially true today, in a fragmented media market that's spilling over with branded communication efforts. Obviously, mass-market communications *can* be meaningful and memorable, but it's getting harder than ever to break through the clutter. Even if a breakthrough happens, consumers who've grown up in the media age view "top-down" communication with suspicion and skepticism. When a message does succeed in getting across, it carries little weight.

Highly charged consumer advocacy through word-of-mouth communication represents the exact opposite. Unlike mass marketing, it's carried "horizontally" from peer to peer, so it has more power and authority. Consumers who believe in certain brand experiences and are vocal about their belief are the carriers. Like a virus, it spreads on contact fast.

Over the last several years, we've observed that, like Cirque du Soleil, the best products and experiences owe their success to word-of-mouth communication.

Data from a recent study by The London School of Economics titled "Advocacy Drives Growth" makes this clear. The study was conducted in the U.K., but its findings have universal implications. It found that positive word-of-mouth predicted sales growth for retail banks, car manufacturers, mobile phone networks, and supermarkets. It also revealed that companies with higher levels of word-of-mouth advocacy grew faster than their competitors and generated greater sales.[1]

Word-of-mouth is valuable currency. Like any currency, we believe that its value can be managed. Build it properly and you have an asset that increases the value of your brand. Ignore it or spend it unwisely and you have a liability—even if you've invested millions above the line.

[1] Marsden, P., Samson, A., and Upton, N. "Advocacy Drives Growth." *Brand Strategy.* Nov/Dec 2005.

Because word-of-mouth advocacy is organic and democratic and because consumers control so much of its power, it can appear scary and unpredictable to marketers. It shouldn't be. What we've seen, time and again, is that positive word-of-mouth happens when a certain number of key factors are present in a brand story. We call these factors the engines of Conversational Capital. By becoming aware of and managing these engines properly, you can turn Conversational Capital into a toolbox that builds value into your product or service.

People are talking. We're writing this because we want you and your brand to be part of the conversation.

WE'RE COMMITTING SUICIDE HERE

We're advertising people, yet, in stumbling upon Conversational Capital, we have unearthed a truth about the branding process that boots the cornerstone of our business right out from under us. The discomfiting thing about Conversational Capital is this: When word-of-mouth works well, traditional advertising and design become much less important. When the engines of Conversational Capital are built into your consumption experience, positive word-of-mouth is likely to follow. So we're stuck with a quandary: Do we spill the beans or shut our mouths and keep billing for the same old same old?

Too bad—Mom always told us to share.

NO, NEVER MIND: WE'RE TOO LAZY!

On second thought, self-immolation requires too much energy. The truth is, advertising people are lazy by nature (otherwise, we'd be novelists, nuclear physicists, or whatever). The second truth about Conversational Capital is that it makes our jobs easier because it turns consumer experiences into tight, compelling stories. And the better the story, the simpler it is to write a great brief, come up with a killer strategy, and produce award-winning creative.

So let's work on that story together. It may be against our essential nature, but we'll do the heavy lifting (promise).

EXCUSE ME, BUT YOU'RE CALLING A LITTLE LATE

We consider ourselves storytellers by trade. We take your consumer experience and distill it into a narrative that's relevant to your target market. Most of the time, however, clients call us too late. By the time they do, they come to us with products and experiences that are already designed and with fully developed stories. And those stories...well, sometimes they're not as compelling as they could be. It's the curse of our business. Conversational Capital enables us to rework with you the narrative that informs your consumer experience, and it helps make that story one that people want to tell.

So, we don't have to spend a lot of time turning the sow's ears into silk purses.

SUMMING UP

- *When products and services become intense experiences, something powerful happens. They become fuel for conversations that consumers engage in to define who they are.*

- *That process turns brands into market leaders. More importantly, what we've observed about market leaders like Cirque du Soleil and others tells why and how it happens.*

- *Turning that process into something you can manage and control is what this book is about.*

QUESTIONS FOR DISCUSSION

Is this just another book about word-of-mouth?

We don't think so. Although this book acknowledges the fundamental importance of word-of-mouth in today's economy, it goes further than anything we've read in describing why and how word-of-mouth happens in the first place.

We think most people will agree, but this book is not intended as a closed discussion. We know there are intelligent and perceptive doubters and nay-sayers out there, and we welcome their points of view. Conversation about Conversational Capital can and will extend outside of this book!

Find out what other people are saying and tell us what you think at www.conversationalcapital.com.

PART ONE

DEFINING CONVERSATIONAL CAPITAL

01.

WHAT IS CONVERSATIONAL CAPITAL?

By studying the activities of category-defining **brands**[2] such as Cirque du Soleil, Apple, adidas, Red Bull, IKEA, method cleaning products, and many others, we've come up with a series of observations that can help generate and spread positive word-of-mouth.

We call these observations Conversational Capital, and they're not just limited to big brand names and international marketers. Some of the world's best word-of-mouth examples are small, local success stories—such as Schwartz's, a much-loved Montréal **smoked meat** restaurant, or an independent artist with a video on YouTube.

What they all have in common is that they are fully endorsed by consumers who share their enthusiasm with their peers. Because word-of-mouth is peer-mediated, it has more authority—this much we know already. However, what Conversational Capital reveals to us is *why* peers talk about an experience to their friends, families, and coworkers.

The short answer is that the experience *means* something to them. This is our first major **insight**. When consumers discover something meaningful in a consumption experience, they are prepared to make the consumption story their own.

This naturally leads to our second major insight. For some time now, marketers have talked about how brands have become

[2] All words highlighted in bold italic in this book are defined in the Glossary and are more extensively discussed in the Blog on www.conversationalcapital.com.

identity markers. What our observations about word-of-mouth tell us is something more: Stories about consumption experiences have become identity *shapers*.

Today's consumers are increasingly developing their own personal narratives, creating and recreating identities for themselves. What they consume and how they consume it are important parts of that **identity-shaping** process. Consumption experiences are substories that they incorporate into their own narratives—the stories they tell that define who they are and how they relate to the world. The more intense and meaningful the substories are, the more likely they are to become part of the larger, personal story.

We call our series of observations Conversational Capital because this storytelling process is a form of powerful currency that transforms the relationship between brand experiences and consumers. In this new type of transaction, marketers provide consumers valuable conversational currency by successfully delivering outstanding and meaningful experiences that help consumers define who they are and where they stand. In return, consumers talk positively about certain experiences and, by extension, increase their value.

You've encountered the process many times. We've all met people who like to talk about their consumption experiences (some at greater length than others). Rather than merely filling gaps in conversation, they are, in essence, talking about themselves. By saying how much they enjoyed Virgin Atlantic's Upper Class service or how delicious Pastis' oysters are, they actually convey that they are interesting jet-setters.

This may all sound very esoteric, but how esoteric can we be? We're marketers! So, as marketers naturally do, we've broken our insights down into an easy-to-understand list of eight "engines" of Conversational Capital: Rituals, Exclusive Product Offering, Myths, Relevant Sensory Oddity, Icons, Tribalism, Endorsement, and Continuity. When some or all of these engines are incorporated into your experience, the result is Conversational

Capital—fuel for stories consumers want to spread to others, the most valuable currency any marketer could hope for.

WE ARE TOTALLY UNORIGINAL

It would be monumentally pretentious of us to claim that we've invented anything new with Conversational Capital. Conversational Capital has been happening for years. We've just given it a name. Great entrepreneurs, such as Cirque du Soleil's Guy Laliberté, have been living by it intuitively long before we came on to the scene. This book is merely the outcome of trying to understand what the truly original have done well already.

So, we're not exactly innovative. Can we still make the claim that we are humble?

SUMMING UP

- *Consumers are likely to become vocal, committed advocates of a consumer experience when it means something to them. If they find the story or brand is telling them something meaningful, they tend to make it part of their own personal narratives.*

- *Personal stories are currency in the modern world. Consumers rely on them to define themselves and project themselves to others. When a brand story becomes part of that currency, the brand's value increases exponentially. That's the "capital" part of Conversational Capital.*

QUESTIONS FOR DISCUSSION

What is the value of Conversational Capital to your business?

You may already wonder what Conversational Capital has to do with you. The answer is that it provides insight into what makes brands have more of an impact and what makes them more memorable across every field of business activity. At this stage, it may sound esoteric, which is why we dig deeper in the following chapters.

We believe our findings are universal. Do you agree or disagree?

Please let us know at www.conversationalcapital.com.

What are you guys talking about?

Throughout this book, we use terms that may be confusing or unclear. To a certain extent, this may result from the fact that we are sailing uncharted waters. Following is a helpful list of terms to make some of the concepts more clear:

- **Salience**—*What do we mean when we speak of salience? It's not a term we've used to sound intellectual. The Oxford English Dictionary defines salience as indicating that which is "the most noticeable or important." In our view, brands and the experiences they render derive their power from salience—from being noticeable and important by virtue of the fact that they hold deep meaning for individuals.*

- **Resonance**—*Resonance occurs when sound vibrates more deeply. Resonant experiences are those that strike a deeper chord with consumers because they provoke us to explore, think, act, and talk. They have* **residual value***.*

- **Residual value**—*Interactions typical of Conversational Capital demonstrate residual value—that is, a quality of being at the forefront of thought even after the immediate encounter ends. That value is leveraged as a currency in the form of conversations that color the identities of their participants.*

02

THE EIGHT ENGINES OF CONVERSATIONAL CAPITAL

The eight engines of Conversational Capital are Rituals, Exclusive Product Offering, Myths, Relevant Sensory Oddity, Icons, Tribalism, Endorsement, and Continuity. These engines can be understood as "experience amplifiers." The presence of one or all of them in a consumption experience helps to make that experience more resonant, richer in *saliency*, more relevant, and more memorable. This, in turn, increases consumer *satisfaction*, which drives positive word-of-mouth consumer support.

RITUALS

Rituals are an essential part of how human beings create and formalize meaning. The presence of ritual marks an experience as deeper in meaning. This is true for consumption experiences, too. Think of the greeters at Wal-Mart and think about people who place a lime wedge into a bottle of Corona beer. These small rituals give the experience of discount shopping and drinking beer a slightly more exalted feeling.

There is a special subset of ritual that occurs so often that we would also like to draw attention to it. This is *initiation*.

Before every Cirque du Soleil show, clowns interact with the crowd as people take their seats, turning innocent audience members into potential comic victims. Espresso connoisseurs finesse the intricacies of their machines to extract the perfect demitasse, crowned by the glory of rich crema foam. All of these are initiations—rites of passage that serve as transitions from the banal and everyday into the meaningful. When products and experiences include rites of initiation, they become more memorable because they are existentially richer.

EXCLUSIVE PRODUCT OFFERING (EPO)

In an era of growing customization, opportunities to own something exclusive increase every day. adidas offers shoppers the means to fashion their own set of shoes in the "mi Originals" section of its stores. No two consumers will have the same list of songs on their iPods. KitchenAid mixers are available online in more than 50 colors and finishes so that you create a kitchen that expresses your personality. You can even put together your own custom blend of vitamins and minerals with Vuru, an online vitamin store. People love to feel unique. Incorporating *EPO* into your experience reinforces the perception that in a world of six billion people, they can.

Over-delivery is another facet of EPO. It defines an aspect of the experience that goes beyond consumer expectations and industry norms, making the experience unique. Think of Volvo's over-arching emphasis on safety or adidas over-delivering on originality in its Originals line that offers 2,400 shoe varieties. Or, simply consider the incredible, above-average service you may have received in a hotel or a restaurant.

MYTHS

Myths are the narratives that become part of the very fabric of a consumption experience because they provide important clues as to what that experience is supposed to mean to us. Michael Dell working out of his college dorm, the stunts and schemes carried out by Richard Branson, Keith Kellogg trying to improve hospital patients' diets—these are now part of the folklore that tell us what Microsoft, Virgin, and Kellogg's stand for, and why their stories should matter to us.

RELEVANT SENSORY ODDITY (RSO)

method cleaning product packages look more like sculpted works of art than packaging. Flower vases in certain hotels designed by Philippe Starck are so large that they seem to defy visual perception. Flight attendants on Air France's *L'Espace Première* don't wear the same perfume, but what if they did? Challenging the senses in such a way is what we call **Relevant Sensory Oddity**. When our senses are presented with something extraordinary, we recognize an experience as special, and we are more likely to talk about that special experience.

ICONS

Icons are signs and symbols that clearly demarcate a consumption experience from any other. These signs and symbols can range from design features such as the three trademark stripes and trefoil on adidas sneakers to familiar logos and product symbols like Mister Clean or the Pillsbury Dough Boy. They can include familiar and distinguishing packaging features such as the Coke bottle and structures such as Cirque du Soleil's familiar blue and yellow big top. Meaningful associations transform signs and symbols from mere product identifiers into components of identity-shaping experiences.

TRIBALISM

Mac users have always thought of themselves as a band apart. Apple has facilitated its desire to gather together members of its own **tribe**. It has helped to create one of the most loyal and vocally supportive user groups on the planet. In addition, it works because our desire to gather into tribes is fundamental to our nature. We like to associate with like-minded people or simply be close to people we find interesting. Being part of a group that we feel is worth belonging to helps us make sense of our lives because it confirms our sense of identity.

ENDORSEMENT

Endorsement is not just about a celebrity lending his or her name to your product or experience, although, under the right circumstances, it can be. Instead, endorsement happens when someone credible speaks up for you. If a trusted authority praises you in a spontaneous and genuine manner, it can have enormous impact because it confirms the relevance of your consumption experience.

CONTINUITY

Your reputation is the result of the relative proximity of three factors to one another, as follows:

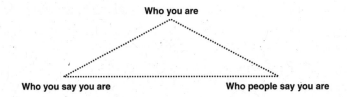

The closer these three are to one another—the more continuous and integrated—the more likely you are to enjoy great word-of-mouth. The farther apart they are, the more likely your reputation is to suffer.

Conversational Capital is about integrity and continuity of image and experience. Word-of-mouth success is the result of effective communication, the inherent value of an experience, and consumer advocacy.

SUMMING UP

The eight engines of Conversational Capital are "experience amplifiers" that make consumption experiences rich in saliency. These eight variables are

- *Rituals*
- *Exclusive Product Offering*
- *Myths*
- *Relevant Sensory Oddity (RSO)*
- *Icons*
- *Tribalism*
- *Endorsement*
- *Continuity*

03

HOW CONVERSATIONAL
CAPITAL WORKS

To best convey how the engines of Conversational Capital help to generate positive word-of-mouth, it isn't sufficient to simply list and describe them. Although Conversational Capital can and should be analyzed intellectually, it is something a consumer *lives*. It is processed existentially to create tropes of meaning that help to shape and confirm one's evolving sense of identity. That's why, whenever we present a new project, we demonstrate how those engines can stoke the emotions and imaginations of consumers as they travel through a brand experience.

By way of example, we invite you to travel through the following brand experiences.

CIRQUE DU SOLEIL

Cirque du Soleil is a company we know well. It also happens to be an ideal example of Conversational Capital at work because it is one of a few consumption experiences that we can think of that encapsulates all eight engines of Conversational Capital.

RITUALS

Essentially, human beings mark out an experience as having greater meaning and weight by ritualizing it in some way.

Above all else, Cirque du Soleil is a powerful and memorable form of live entertainment. From concerts to football games, gathering together to watch live entertainment has become a widespread modern ritual—a form of modern congregation with echoes of religious ritual. Think of fans flicking on their lighters (or lately cell phones) like votive candles or singing together and waving their hands in unison.

Cirque du Soleil takes the ritual nature of live performance and builds on it in two important ways:

- As the audience settles into its seats, clowns and characters from a show emerge and playfully interact with the crowd. They choose certain members of the audience and get them to take part in some bit of foolery. Usually, the person chosen is a good sport and participates enthusiastically. Sometimes, people resist, and become the butt of jokes. In either case, the rest of the audience laughs. And yet, as they laugh, a huge number of people in the audience are most likely thinking, "Oh, please, don't pick me."

Whatever the reaction of individual crowd members, this pre-show clowning is an *initiation*. Initiation rituals have been part of human experience throughout history and across cultures. They create a clear line between the ordinary and the sublime. The initiation at Cirque du Soleil shows does this by breaking down the line between audience and performer. The performer becomes part of the audience, the audience becomes part of the show, and everyone is exalted. In the space of a few minutes, we are taken out of our daily consciousness and arbitrary classifications, and we are made more receptive. We are brought into a newly rarified sphere, that of the show that is about to unfold.

- At most Cirque shows, when the show officially begins, the cast and characters appear among the audience and make their way to the stage in a formal procession.

  Like initiation, processions are Ritual Behavior 101 (think of wedding and funeral processions). They instantly communicate a key message of rituals: "We have all come together for a special event." A procession is like a line drawn in the sand: It indicates that the triviality of daily reality has been put on hold for awhile and opens the door to something else—something more meaningful and memorable.

EXCLUSIVE PRODUCT OFFERING (EPO)

In a world of mass production, we love to be reminded that we are individuals. Each one of us has our own taste, perspective, and history. When we have experiences that confirm our individuality, they stand out.

Because Cirque du Soleil is a form of live entertainment, each performance of a show is special and distinct. Like any live act, it changes in some small way from one performance to the next. The show you see will be slightly different from the show I see—so you and I will each "own" the show in our respective ways.

What makes each Cirque performance even more exclusive than other live events is what might be called a "democratic" approach to staging. Cirque shows consist of a series of circus numbers connected by an overriding theme or mood. Yet, when each number takes place, it is never the only thing happening on stage. On different parts of the stage, characters respond to the main action or begin an action of their own. The result is that the audience member isn't forced to focus his attention on one thing alone. Each audience member, focusing on different aspects of the staging at different times, edits together their own, distinct sequence of events.

What's more, the narratives and themes of each show are loosely stated. The audience members are invited in to shape their own meaning, to create their own story from key characters and plot points.

This democracy of action and reaction is entirely intended. The end result is a highly individualized experience of the show. When we sit together in a movie theater, we watch more or less the same film. None of us sees exactly the same Cirque du Soleil show.

OVER-DELIVERY

Over-delivery sets an experience apart by taking the idea of customer satisfaction and lifting it to an entirely new level. Successful marketers live according to the principle that you have to exceed customer expectations.

Cirque du Soleil consistently over-delivers in terms of acrobatic performance. Each show features new and more thrilling numbers, defying audiences to guess what to expect next. Even in the more established shows, the artists and acrobats systematically push themselves to a more perfect performance, night after night. Each performance is videotaped, and after each show, acrobats and coaches examine what to the untrained eye might be minutiae. Where could they have done better? How?

Most audience members have not asked for this. They are more than satisfied by what they have seen. And yet, Cirque lives to push the envelope, to take audience members where they never expected to go. This renders the experience more than merely satisfying. It makes it meaningful, memorable, and singular.

MYTHS

Myths are narratives that encapsulate the essential meaning of an experience. When a myth is powerful enough, its presence is felt with varying degrees of intensity throughout an experience.

Guy Laliberté, Cirque's founder, began his career by entertaining crowds on the street as a fire breather. He came up with his company's name while on the Big Island in Hawaii. He was looking for a symbol that he thought would incorporate the spirit of youth, fire, and optimism he wanted his company to stand for. Looking up, he found that symbol in the sun. In addition to its name ("soleil" is French for sun), much of Cirque du Soleil's visual iconography is solar. So, even if we don't know the details of Cirque du Soleil's *founding myth*, we are reminded of it whenever and wherever we encounter the company.

RELEVANT SENSORY ODDITY (RSO)

Our minds and our hearts delight in surprise. Perhaps because the way we live demands routine and repetition that drain meaning out of existence, we tend to remember and speak about experiences that break the mold. The more those breakthrough moments excite our senses, the more "sticky" they become. Cirque du Soleil enjoys excellent word–of–mouth because surprise and delight are what they do best.

Cirque du Soleil, is, above all things, a purveyor of live circus entertainment. We are (perhaps too) accustomed to seeing the impossible happen on our film and television screens. Yet, we are always conscious that the amazing things we see are fake, the result of special effects. At a Cirque show, the impossible, death-defying acts we witness are *actually happening*. And rather than simply taking them in through the relatively sanitized and heavily visual media of film and television, we are witnessing them in an environment where all our senses are awake. We not only actually see these stunts, but we also hear them, smell them, taste them, and, in some magical way, feel them in the charged electric air of the live performance.

By insisting on a high level of physical performance, Cirque du Soleil delivers these sensory thrills like no one else. With each show, it pushes the envelope of the seemingly impossible further. KÀ, a permanent show in Las Vegas, takes place on a moving stage that, at times, is perpendicular to the floor. Performers literally run up and down walls, defying our senses. In O, another Cirque show in Vegas, performers walk and dance across water. A man, engulfed in flames, calmly reads a newspaper.

Unsurprisingly, challenging sensory boundaries gets people talking.

ICONS

Cirque presents customers with a strikingly rousing icon: a sign encapsulating the meaning of its live entertainment experience.

Cirque du Soleil's principal icon is its Big Top. Most of Cirque du Soleil's touring shows perform under a signature blue and yellow striped Big Top. When set up in a major center, the structure is unmistakable; it commands our attention. It signifies that the landscape of the city has changed—something vital and interesting has come to town. Often, it is set up in parts of town that are less traveled, unexpected, and surprising. This is intentional, and it tells people that Cirque du Soleil is about renewal, reinvention, and hope.

The image of the Big Top is powerful. For centuries before Cirque du Soleil existed, the circus was a symbol of "the other," of a life outside the ordinary, and an alternative to the daily grind (People dreamed and still dream of "running away with the circus"). By modifying the Big Top and giving it a new visual identity, Cirque du Soleil built on the strength of that icon and vested it with new power.

The icon is now so powerful and recognizable that it appears in various forms throughout Cirque's communications and merchandise. Seeing it, the consumer automatically understands it as part of a larger story.

TRIBALISM

Touring Cirque productions are cleverly arranged so that there is plenty of time for people to meet before the show starts and plenty of space to mingle in. Weather permitting, crowds gather outside the Big Top, and the atmosphere quickly becomes that of a pleasant outdoor cocktail party. As you arrive at the show, you can't help but look at the assembled crowd and think, "Well, here we all are. I know that person, and that person...." If you don't know people personally, you are immediately aware of similarities in income level, cultural leanings, and taste (Cirque tickets are a premium good, and the shows tend to attract a more moneyed crowd).

The sense of being part of a tribe, then, begins almost right away. We have spoken previously about the ritual sense of procession as artists begin the show and about interactive clowning before the show starts. These and other elements of the show bring Cirque's undercurrent of tribalism even closer to the surface. The intent of the shows is to break down the line between audience and performers. Essentially, we are invited into the Cirque tribe.

For those who become true believers and Cirque brand ambassadors, the experience sticks. They become dedicated fans and connect with other fans in as many ways as they can, most recently and effectively through Internet chat rooms, fan clubs, and user groups.

ENDORSEMENT

When consumers find an experience meaningful, they connect with it. The more that experience has meaning for them, the deeper the connection—until consumer and experience are connected almost neurally. When that connection happens, consumers become endorsers. Ask yourself who the 100 most influential endorsers for your experience would be. Establish a neural connection with them, and you create cascading endorsement.

This is what happened with Cirque du Soleil. Cirque was a moderately successful company until it first played in Los Angeles in 1986. As it happened, Cirque's 100 or so important *influencers*—show business tastemakers—discovered Cirque du Soleil there at the same time. They spontaneously became endorsers, and Cirque's exponential growth began.

To this day, permanent and touring Cirque shows often welcome influential celebrities and dignitaries backstage. Many are surprised to hear that these visits are treated with discretion, rather than routinely turned into photo or video opportunities. Instead, news of such visits spreads through word-of-mouth.

Because these endorsements are unheralded, they have more credibility and impact. The cultural elite, we reason, are show business experts. They have experienced more than the average audience member and, therefore, must be tougher to please. Yet, they become fans and supporters of Cirque spontaneously, without long-term contracts and remuneration. Under these conditions, we tell ourselves that if they appreciate Cirque du Soleil, there must be something to this new mixture of circus and theater.

CONTINUITY

Reputation is all about continuity between who you are, who you say you are, and who people say you are. It's helpful to think of these as points on a triangle:

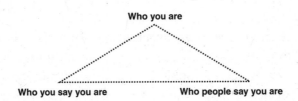

The farther apart these three points are, the more problematic your reputation will be. The closer together they are, the more likely you are to enjoy word-of-mouth success. Ideally, they would converge at the same point, like so:

Having a "small triangle" essentially means that there is integrity and continuity between your experience, your image, and what people say about you. This kind of reputation creates a positive feedback loop that is vital to nourish and protect.

Cirque du Soleil enjoys this kind of reputation, benefiting from infectious fan support and enthusiasm. And it responds to the positive pressure created by positive word-of-mouth by consistently providing a highly engaging experience.

Avoiding empty promises and unfulfilled expectations, it has drawn new customers to the brand while maintaining the valuable relationship it enjoys with brand ambassadors.

IKEA

Clearly, Cirque du Soleil can tell a convincing, memorable, and meaningful story. And it should—its core business, after all, is spectacle. This might beg the question: Is it possible to see the engines of Conversational Capital at work outside of show business—say, in retail? The answer is a resounding "yes." IKEA's international success provides an excellent example.

The entire IKEA experience is informed by a founding myth. IKEA's *positioning* statement exclaims that it is "Your partner in better living. We do our part; you do yours. Together we save money." This is fitting for a company whose founding was informed by a maverick sense of self-reliance and frugality, and whose continuing goal is to improve living conditions for the masses.

IKEA was founded in Sweden in 1943 by Ingvar Kamprad, then 17. The retail behemoth grew from inauspicious beginnings, trading in pens, wallets, picture frames, watches, jewelry, and nylon stockings. Its mission was to sell anything people had a need for that could be moved for a better price. The eccentric founder has built a reputation for being parsimonious. He rides public transit to work, and when he drives, it's a 15-year-old Volvo. He flies economy, and when he stays in hotels, he is rumored to bring sodas from nearby convenience stores to avoid expensive minibar products. He asks workers to write on both sides of paper. He is known to enter IKEA stores for a cheap meal. He buys his Christmas presents and wrapping paper…after Christmas.

His frugality, however, does not extend to philanthropy. Kamprad's holding company operates a prominent charitable organization. The firm and its outlets also have an extensive history of supporting local communities. IKEA is dedicated to "better living" across every aspect of its business operations. Consumers are clearly drawn by a lifestyle offering that will increase their comfort and sense of style without compromising their finances. Employees also benefit from IKEA's largesse. IKEA employee lounge and rest areas feature comfortable couches, music, television, Internet kiosks, quiet rooms, and shower facilities. For food and refreshment, IKEA Canada offers free coffee and tea and an outdoor eating area featuring a barbeque. The company has a full-service onsite cafeteria that offers subsidized meals (a sandwich costs $3.50), healthy menu items, special diet menus, and an exceptional Swedish meatball dinner. Other work area amenities include cutting-edge workstations, onsite fitness facilities at some locations, and a resource room featuring televisions, computers, and reading materials.

Many retail experiences are discontinuous. Clearly, the IKEA experience is not. IKEA represents a completely holistic and integrated approach that sets a standard in retail: *continuity*. Indeed, continuity at retail is a stated goal at IKEA. They put it this way (the italics are ours): "IKEA aim[s] to look after our customers by planning for their needs. Not only do we provide inspiration and ideas, but we *also encourage people to touch, feel, and use the products on display to see how they would fit into their own home.*"

IKEA products are famously displayed in model bedrooms, living rooms, kitchens, and offices. This makes it easy for customers to imagine how a purchased item or items will fit together in their own living or working spaces.

The IKEA experience is also marked by a distinct sense of ritual at various stages of the shopping experience. This is not a retail space where you walk up and down aisles mechanically. Instead, markings on the floor lead us on a continuous, winding procession through various spaces designed for one type of living or another. IKEA also presents consumers with various levels of initiation. Rather than being numbered or simply labeled, IKEA products are named in a Swedish-inspired Esperanto that challenges consumers. If you can tell a Gutvik from a Verktyg from a Hemlig, you are truly one of the initiated. The sense of ritual initiation continues as you pick various items for purchase. Do you pick them up on the spot and put them in your cart? Do you search through a warehouse space adjacent to the cash? Do you wait in yet another warehouse space *after* you've paid, as you must for some items? Or, do you forego all of that and make a special order first. Only an experienced IKEA customer can tell you for sure. Finally, IKEA is a staple of the modern "D.I.Y." culture. Buy furniture at IKEA, and you have to assemble it yourself. They provide the tools, and many customers have drawers full of Allen keys (and maybe leftover parts) to show for it. But after you bring that item home, you're on your own. With a house full of IKEA furniture, you have not only demonstrated taste and style, but also a certain amount of skill, coordination, and self-mastery. How's *that* for initiation?

The *"yourself"* aspect of "do it yourself" is a key component of the IKEA experience, which naturally makes it a hallmark of EPO. My IKEA is not yours, or his, or hers. Rather, it is a reflection of my individualized tastes and needs—EPO. Almost everything at IKEA is about tailoring design around you. From interchangeable table legs, to multipatterned slipcovers, to modular kitchens and baths, IKEA products are about facilitating *personalization*.

As mentioned previously, EPO is not simply about personalization.

Experiences can also stand out because of over-delivery on one aspect of experience or another. IKEA constantly seeks to over-deliver on various aspects of the retail experience. Consider the following:

- On average, its stores stock 12,000 products, and those products are constantly tweaked by IKEA's own cadre of noteworthy industrial designers.

- The IKEA catalogue reaches 175 million households around the world, translated in 17 languages.

- And now, IKEA lets you stay in its stores overnight! Writes Gwladys Fouché of the *Guardian*: "Later this month, IKEA Norway will let shoppers sleep overnight in one of its two Oslo warehouses, an operation that will last a week." "It will be like an alternative hostel," said company spokesman Frode Ullebust. "There will be the regular dormitory with lots of beds stacked up together. We will also have a bridal suite with a round bed and a hanging chandelier and the luxury suite, where customers can enjoy breakfast in bed," he said. "Family rooms will also be available for parents and children to join into the IKEA fun. None of the guests will be charged for their stay."[3]

Mr. Ullebust said that, as far as he knew, this was IKEA's first foray into the hotel business. "Every night, the 30 lucky few will stack up on meatballs, Norwegian salmon, and cranberry mousse, as IKEA is offering free dinner and breakfast at the usual canteen."

Whereas Brits may associate the Swedish furniture giant with screaming kids, traffic jams in the parking lot, and an occasional riot when a new warehouse opens, it seems Norwegians see a trip to IKEA as the ultimate tourist attraction.

---

[3] Fouche, Gwladys. "Check in to the IKEA bridal suite for a flat-pack honeymoon." *The Guardian*. London. July 13, 2007.

Approximately 900,000 visitors visit IKEA during the summer holidays. "It's more than one of the biggest attractions in Norway, the Holmenskollen ski jump, gets in one year," claimed Mr. Ullebust.

How about RSO? So many aspects of the IKEA experience challenge our senses and revise our expectations about what a retail experience should be like. Following are some RSO features:

- The smell of meatballs and lingonberries

- The children's playroom

- The lifestyle pod meets warehouse design of the store

- The aforementioned product names, such as labels from a dream in which you recognize a language but can't quite make it out

- The instructions in their generic, confounding, text-free glory

The IKEA experience is also marked by the notable presence of *icons*. They start with the 362-page catalogue and extend to the store. Ranging in the hundreds of thousands of square-feet, IKEA stores are some of the largest retail buildings to be found anywhere—bigger even than a Super Wal-Mart. When inside, you find yet more signs and symbols. From the highly symbolic Volkswagen Beetle often parked in the entrance, to the yellow and blue bags that visitors carry around so dutifully; from the yellow arrows guiding you through the maze to the nondescript brown boxes stacked to the ceiling in the warehouse self-serve area, and from the bagged meatballs to the photos of half-shaven poodles in its catalogues, IKEA icons get people talking.

And talk they clearly do. IKEA's success is clearly a result of both tribalism and endorsement. IKEA furniture has become nearly ubiquitous among upwardly mobile and style-conscious members of the international middle-class. IKEA has become more than a place to shop: It has become a destination where members of this tribe congregate in an act of communal self-affirmation. As writer Stephen Moss puts it, "IKEA is preoccupied with relationships. Whereas traditional stores have usually appealed to individual consumers, IKEA wants to attract families or groups of friends. You often see not just couples trailing around, but the rest of the extended family, too: It is the modern equivalent of the day at the seaside in the 50s and 60s, a chance for the family to do something communally.

"But IKEA wants to have it both ways. It knows that the nuclear family is disintegrating, so it seeks to appeal beyond its boundaries. Last year it ran an ad campaign, tagged 'Make a fresh start,' that encouraged people in failing marriages to get divorced. It pitches directly to remarrying couples, to single parents (men as well as women), and to gay couples, who feature prominently in its advertising. Part of its optimism lies in a belief that the right relationship can be found; that dud relationships should be ditched; that you have to be yourself."[4]

A more specifically delineated tribe has formed around IKEA's iconic catalogue. Fans of the IKEA catalogue rejoice at its annual issue. It is produced in 38 editions, in 17 languages, and for 28 countries. The Canadian Television Network (CTV) claims that "IKEA's publications have developed an almost cult-like following online. Readers have found all kinds of strange tidbits, including mysterious cat pictures, apparent Mickey Mouse references, and weird books wedged into the many shelves that clutter the catalogues."[5] There's even a Facebook group that celebrates the controversial opening photo of a dog in the 2006 IKEA catalogue.

Clearly, IKEA isn't just about what you buy. It's about how you live: And it has become so thoroughly integrated into the lifestyles of so many that it has naturally become a hallmark of peer endorsement. Most new customers at IKEA go because

---

[4] Kamprad, Ingvar. "A Furniture Dealer's Testament." Cited in Moss, Stephen. "The Gospel According to IKEA." *The Guardian*, June 26, 2000.

[5] Ibid.

they have heard about it from a friend or have seen how an IKEA product has become seamlessly integrated into that friend's life. IKEA does invest in mainstream advertising, but when a company has as many brand ambassadors as IKEA does, you wonder why if does so at all.

SCHWARTZ'S—MONTRÉAL'S HEBREW DELICATESSEN

Cirque du Soleil's and IKEA's success at generating and sustaining positive word-of-mouth is undeniable. We hope that reading through the last few pages has helped you to see how what we call the engines of Conversational Capital have been part of the equation.

But that begs an important question: Is the presence of Conversational Capital limited to international purveyors of live entertainment or global retail success stories? Our analysis of Schwartz's, a Montréal landmark beloved by locals and tourists alike, indicates otherwise. Indeed, the engines of Conversational Capital can be discerned across the entire spectrum of consumer experience. In later chapters, we'll demonstrate this in detail. For now, let's concentrate on this humble—but much talked about—cultural institution.

THE SCHWARTZ'S EXPERIENCE

Schwartz's is a tiny delicatessen with plain white walls, simple wooden tables set up in rows seating six persons each, and minimal decor. It could be any local joint in a town like yours. On one side, as you enter, you will note a counter that seats a handful of customers. Behind the counter hang large slabs of smoked, spiced beef brisket. On the wall opposite the counter, there are pictures of the (now late) original owner and his friends and family, photos of famous visitors, and framed restaurant reviews. Waiters in plain white shirts serve items from a limited menu in an unpretentious manner: mostly smoked meat sandwiches on rye bread with side orders of pickles and French fries. Some customers also order rib steak, served with an entree of liver and a small sausage. Chicken is on the menu, but after decades of regular visits, we have never seen anyone eat it.

It doesn't look like much, and yet Schwartz's enjoys incredible international word-of-mouth and an extremely loyal customer base. It has never employed **mass-marketing** techniques, and yet it continually draws in new customers while retaining its existing clientele. Show up any day of the year at lunchtime or dinner, and you are likely to stand in line outside on Saint-Laurent Boulevard.

Ah yes, the ever-present line. This is your first indicator of what has been behind Schwartz's tremendous word-of-mouth success.

Being part of the ever-present lineup at Schwartz's has taken on the flavor of *ritual*. It is never pleasant to stand in line, particularly in Montréal's notorious subzero weather, but at Schwartz's, standing in line has become for many an integral part of the consumption experience. We believe that this is because standing in line has become a form of *initiation*, which we have described as a special subset of ritual. You stand in line at Schwartz's because you feel it will be worth it. Braving the cold and the crowd prepares you for the warmth and welcome inside. Being ready to stand in line also demonstrates that you are in the know: There are other purveyors of smoked meat in Montréal, but not one quite like Schwartz's. When you have stood in line, you have become one of the initiated elect.

Standing in line also serves another function. It reinforces a feeling of *tribalism*. There is an easy familiarity and sense of belonging in the Schwartz's line, because there is a shared understanding among the people there of the value of the experience they are waiting for. Standing in line on Saint-Laurent Boulevard feels urban and cool, nothing like waiting for a table at, say, Appleby's or Howard Johnson's. It creates the sense that the anticipation and ritualism of going to Schwartz's must be worth it.

The seating arrangement at the restaurant is another aspect of the Schwartz's experience that fosters tribalism. Unless you are dining with five other people, chances are good you will be seated at a long table or counter with strangers. However, an instant connection with that stranger is possible because of an assumption of shared taste and "insider" knowledge. As with any tribe, there are varying degrees of belonging: Longtime customers sit with "newbies," never shy to share their insight into how best to order a meal.

The pictures on the wall are testament to the strong presence of *endorsement*. As Schwartz's website proudly proclaims, "Schwartz's smoked meat and steaks have been enjoyed by rock stars, movie stars, and heads of state. You are in the company of Céline Dion, Hank Aaron, Nana Mouskouri, Jean Chrétien, Ken Dryden, Jerry Lewis, Guy Lafleur, Jean Béliveau, Rusty Staub, Halle Berry, Angelina Jolie, Tim Allen, The Rolling Stones...." Note that each of these Taste Makers simply showed up: They weren't hired. Their endorsement is natural, organic, and unforced. You might also note that the endorsers come from all walks of life: entertainment, sports, and politics. Were Schwartz's to have deliberately chosen 100 influencers to reach people across the consumer spectrum, they couldn't have done much better than this list of people.

Schwartz's provides a wonderful example of *Relevant Sensory Oddity* (RSO). Come into Schwartz's from a wintry street and you are surrounded by warmth, and more importantly, the transporting aroma of grilled meat and spices. The aforementioned slabs of smoked meat stand out like works of art, even more so when out-of-town visitors leave the restaurant with a recently purchased slab in their arms.

It is highly unlikely that anyone present in the restaurant has just walked in by chance. They have all, in one way or another, been drawn here by Schwartz's continuity between what it promises and what it delivers. In this deli's case, that reputation is stellar: "A Beef on Rye to Freeze to Death for!" says the *Financial Times*. "The best place in the Milky Way to sample smoked meat sandwiches!" says *Time Magazine*. "When you're in Montréal, you must go to Schwartz's," enthuses the *New York Times*. "A Montréal legend for 75 years. So what's the big deal?

It's the *viande fumée* that overwhelms two slices of rye," explains *National Geographic*. The reputation survives because one's experience of Schwartz's lives up to the good things people have to say about it.

Schwartz's is also a wonderful example of *exclusive product offering*. Smoked meat is already a hard-to-experience item (it truly exists in only Montréal; pastrami, its closest relative, is nothing like it). Schwartz's is recognized as having the best smoked meat—and there is only one Schwartz's. In fact, offered the chance to expand into another location, the owners have always declined. This has been a wise choice because, by keeping Schwartz's small and in a single location, it has reinforced a feeling of **exclusivity**. If you have managed to make it to Schwartz's, you truly own an experience that can't be replicated anywhere else (it's *yours*).

The deli, with its classic and unpretentious décor and service, has become an *icon* of authenticity and tradition.

Lastly, because of its continued presence in Montréal for decades, Schwartz's has achieved—and maintains—the status of *myth*. This is partly because smoked meat, its main product, is mythical in origin. There is conjecture that the recipe was brought to Montréal by Romanian Jews who settled in the neighborhood around Schwartz's, but no one is certain. The exact mechanics of its preparation are a well-kept secret.

No wonder people talk about it.

SEAMLESS AND HOLISTIC

The three cases presented here are seemingly divergent. They are united by one intimately shared value. In each case, the engines of Conversational Capital have been worked into the experience seamlessly and holistically. They are an integral part of the experience and not just applied to it like rabbit ears to a chicken.

This is important because it tells us that Conversational Capital is about continuity, depth, and resonance. As you'll see in the next chapter, this is a key reason why Conversational Capital works.

SUMMING UP

We have examined three market leaders from diverse fields of activity and have seen the same principles at work. The consumer experiences offered by Cirque du Soleil, IKEA, and Schwartz's Delicatessen are amplified and made more resonant by what we call "The Engines of Conversational Capital." These engines can be seen as carriers or drivers of the brand story.

The Engines are:

- *Rituals*
- *Exclusive Product Offering (EPO)*
- *Myths*
- *Relevant Sensory Oddity (RSO)*
- *Icons*
- *Tribalism*
- *Endorsement*
- *Continuity*

QUESTIONS FOR DISCUSSION

Did the cases cited know about Conversational Capital when they designed their products and experiences?

Clearly not. Each of the examples cited is a case of original, entrepreneurial genius. The experiences have come to contain the engines of Conversational Capital organically. We simply observed their presence and are trying to understand how they work.

We believe that through this understanding, we can consciously replicate what others developed intuitively. Do you think such a thing is possible? Challenge us online.

04.

WHY CONVERSATIONAL
CAPITAL WORKS

Conversational Capital works because of a simple five-part equation:

1. Consumers are presented with more choices than they have ever had. One could argue that they are presented with too many choices.

2. In the presence of time constraints, consumers are now more sophisticated and discriminating than they have ever been.

3. As they become more sophisticated, consumers naturally turn to experiences that are richer in meaning and cohesion.

4. These rich experiences are what get talked about most.

5. Incorporating the engines of Conversational Capital into consumer offerings increases meaning and cohesion.

It's a simple equation. Understanding and managing all the factors in the equation is a little more complex. That's why we wrote this book.

As we emerge from an era of homogenized, incremental brand experiences, consumers are hungry for change. Conversational Capital enables companies to deliver that change in the form of rich, powerful, meaningful experiences. Conversational Capital increases the residual value of consumption experiences.

We have a saying, "A three-hour meal in a good restaurant can last a lifetime…"—if that meal becomes the source of stories. If an experience is rich enough to give us a tale to tell, we will want to return again and again, as people have returned to Cirque du Soleil, IKEA, and Schwartz's over the years. Conversational Capital helps you craft those stories and maximize the residual value of the resulting experience.

If you are a marketing professional, that's important because it gives you new power. Conversational Capital employs marketing techniques, theories, and most importantly, creativity to reengineer brand experiences from the ground up. It turns product design and product marketing into components of an integrated process—something they should have been all along.

HEY, MARKETING PEOPLE:
WE'VE HAD IT WITH YOU BEING LEFT OUT

Marketers get no respect, especially marketing vice presidents. If you're lucky, you get called into the room where your company managers are discussing a product or experience after everyone else has had a go at it. The guy from the finance department, the woman from operations, and the Director of Human Resources get their say first. This is a shame. As a marketer, you not only bring real insight into product development, but you also make a significant contribution to the product story that is at the heart of Conversational Capital because you know what's meaningful to your market. We hope this book can change things for the marketer. Conversational Capital reveals that product development and marketing should always be an integrated process. When you speak the language, you should be among the first in, not the last.

Keep that in mind the next time you see the Human Resources dude hogging all the donuts.

CURRENCY FOR THE HIGH-SALIENCY AGE

There won't be any turning back. We have moved from a top-down, mass-market approach to a horizontally organized, participatory trope of social organization in which the individual consumer is empowered as never before.

We have moved from what we call the "low saliency" experience era to the "high saliency" experience age. By saliency, we mean impact, depth of consumer interaction with the product or message, and meaning. The more an experience is salient, the greater its capacity to reach, involve, and move the consumer. Low saliency was a hallmark of the mass-market era. High saliency is where Conversational Capital lives.

When an experience is high in saliency, consumers live it more vividly. It becomes more important to them. In the best cases, these experiences become the building blocks of how consumers think about themselves and define themselves to others in conversation. In other words, stories about these experiences become a form of *social currency*, which makes them especially valuable.

Generally speaking, mass-media communications are low in saliency. In a large-scale media campaign, reach and frequency are maximized to ensure a relatively uncompelling message gets to as many people as possible and enough times for that message to embed itself. In other words, say it everywhere and say it so often that defenseless consumers get the message.

The problem is, even at this level, mass marketing loses its power. It's not just that most people believe that most ads are lame. They are right, after all. The issue is that these lame ads are repeated far too often. Consumers are afflicted by a form of "frequency overload." They can live with the pedestrian nature of most advertising, but not with the advertiser's resolve to hammer them again and again with the same low-saliency message.

In spite of this, every organization cleaving to the traditional and still generally accepted mass-marketing paradigm leverages the same strategy. It's crowded out there, and consumers being human have a limited capacity to absorb messages, forcing users of mass media to keep their messages simple.

So, although mass marketing is typically effective at generating product **awareness** (buy Detox Detergent), it is not particularly useful at inducing product comprehension (its enzymatic action breaks down stains), much less facilitating meaningful product-consumer interaction (join the Dirty Laundry Club, Detox Detergent's online user group).

In this paradigm, it is understood that, after awareness is generated, consumer interest and involvement are assured through other means, such as "below-the-line" marketing communication efforts (direct marketing, sales force training, sampling, point-of-sale trials, and so on).

Look at this way of doing things closely enough, and you can see that the intensity and meaning of the product-consumer relationship increase in direct proportion to its place "above" or "below" the line. Mass-media advertising, at the top of the funnel where big dollars are spent, is the lowest in saliency. At the spout of the funnel, where few marketing dollars are spent, the product-consumer relationship is highest in saliency. This is the one-to-one level where marketer and customer interact directly and where the closest contact is made.

Isn't this picture fundamentally skewed? Shouldn't marketing efforts be as meaningful and effective as possible and as often as possible? The marketers we observe and admire would say, "Of course they should," and they would act accordingly.

Take, for example, Red Bull. Red Bull has staked out international leadership by making intense experiences an important part of the marketing process. Consumers discover Red Bull products through high-intensity events, such as Flügtag, a contest in which makers of home-made flying machines plummet 30 feet off a pier into the water below. They are also the originators of Crashed Ice, a sporting event that combines bobsledding and ice hockey with roller derby. Product sampling is carried out by Mobile Energy Teams who target new customers in key areas. These efforts are never simple. Rather, they carry an aura of excitement, danger, and irreverence.

Flügtag and Crashed Ice are both rituals. Red Bull's mobile energy team invites potential users to partake in shared tribalism. Red Bull's cans are examples of Relevant Sensory Oddity (RSO). Everywhere we turn, we see a definite correlation between higher salience and the presence of the engines of Conversational Capital.

1984: A HALLMARK OF MASS COMMUNICATION HIGH SALIENCE

In *Buzzmarketing: Get People to Talk About Your Stuff*, Mark Hughes points to a commercial aired by Apple during the 1984 Super Bowl telecast as a historical example of how to generate great word-of-mouth.[6] Produced for a staggering (at the time) $1.6 million, the 58-second spot was directed by Ridley Scott. It featured breath-taking visuals and a resonant allegory.

The futuristic dystopia inspired directly by George Orwell's *1984* features an army of grey-skinned, bald drones gathering to watch a speech barked at them by a menacing Big Brother figure on a giant screen. As the drones watch spellbound, a magnificent female athlete runs from a group of helmeted paratroopers. Before they can catch her, she heroically hurls a hammer into the screen. It explodes, spraying light onto the open-mouthed drones. A message then scrolls up the screen. An announcer reads the message, "On January 24, Apple will introduce Macintosh. And you'll see why 1984 won't be like '1984.'"

The spot was a clear articulation of the self-expression and freedom that Apple is about—values that remain as true today as they were more than 20 years ago. 1984 was embraced by millions and hailed by critics as a classic. It aired only once.

According to conventional advertising rules, the spot was an exercise in folly. Far more money went into its production than into media buying (a reversal of standard practice). Steve Jobs was almost removed from the Apple board for supporting it. However, he was absolutely right to do what he did.

[6] Hughes, Mark. *Buzzmarketing: Get People to Talk About Your Stuff*. New York. 2007.

WHEN WE WROTE THIS BOOK, WE WERE NAKED

As you read this book, can you picture a group of men in their 40s naked? Do you want to picture this? Does it make you think about yourself naked? Snapping you out of your mode is a form of RSO. We hope that it makes reading this book more memorable and meaningful.

Conversational Capital equals higher saliency. That's our basic formula, and if we don't work it into the book ourselves, we're not walking the talk.

Yes, the naked thing is relevant (not just sensorially odd) because we lay ourselves bare here.

Apple's agency Chiat\Day had crafted a marketing phenomenon that resulted in cascading word-of-mouth. The spot generated an incredible amount of free publicity; it was rebroadcast on every news program that night. It became the subject of water-cooler conversation everywhere. All of the word-of-mouth, we are sure you may have noted, came about at no added expense to Apple.

Hughes describes the word-of-mouth generating power of the spot well when he writes: "Apple Computer got everyone talking about its computer in America because it gave people a story to talk about…people talked about that amazing commercial, about the audacity of poking IBM in the chest, about George Orwell's book, *1984*, about the new era of Big Brother and how there might be a mini-microphone recording their every word at the water cooler right then and there."

Nevertheless, like so many self-described "buzz marketers," Hughes misses the point of why the ad had the impact it did. He seems to think that the ad's impact had everything to do with surface message and little to do with the product being advertised. He writes, "On the day after the Super Bowl, can you imagine people talking about a computer? Water-cooler conversation centered around MIPS or DRAM? Absolutely not. Boooorrring!" Hughes continues, "The story is not Apple's technology, all its MIPS and DRAM crap…not the product, not its attributes."

Clearly, Hughes seems to think that the word-of-mouth success of the *1984* spot had everything to do with sizzle and nothing to do with steak. We don't think this is accurate.

The spot was intensely memorable and rich with meaning. Looking at it now, we observe that it was powered by the engines of Conversational Capital. Because of how it looked and sounded, it jarred viewers with a sense of RSO (they could justifiably ask themselves, "What exactly are we looking at here: an ad, a film, a promo for a television show?"). With its use of the Big Brother and female athlete figures—opposing a symbol of oppressive collectivism against powerful individuality—it makes good use of icons. Finally, because it borrows so much from Orwell and the *1984* mythos, it makes good use of myth.

Why does this prove Hughes wrong? The engines of Conversational Capital do not work unless they are tied, ultimately, to a satisfactory and truly significant consumer experience. In essence, what the spot promised, Apple delivered—perhaps not at the level of MIPS and DRAM "crap" (which are product features sans crap), but in terms of how it felt to use the product (the net benefit). This historic spot provides a wonderful example of absolute continuity between **brand promise**, communication, and brand experience. The spot could have been **bombastic** and hollow, but it wasn't. The first Macintosh computers delivered the revolutionary design and freedom that the spots promised. Because of this, talk about the product became unquestionable: It practiced what the spot preached.

This is an important point because word-of-mouth experts such as Hughes so often appear to make the same mistake. They equate **buzz** with word-of-mouth, and the two are not the same thing at all.

SUMMING UP

- *Consumers today are more sophisticated than ever and have more choice. Faced with a barrage of options, they tend to gravitate to experiences rich in meaning and saliency.*

- *These experiences get talked about because they provide fuel for stories that consumers use to define themselves. These stories are a new form of social currency. When a brand becomes currency by providing Conversational Capital, it leads.*

- *The challenge for marketers in the post mass-media age is to remain salient throughout the product design and marketing processes because consumers increasingly demand it.*

QUESTIONS FOR DISCUSSION

How much change does Conversational Capital require?

The answer varies, depending on who you are and what you do. You may be one of the brand leaders cited in this book or someone whose praises are sung at conversationalcapital.com. Or, you may be at the opposite end of the scale altogether: No one speaks about your brand, or if they do, it's in a bad way.

Wherever you stand, we believe that the process of implementing Conversational Capital needs to be comprehensive and continuous, even for leaders, because its implications are deep and far reaching. It may involve the alteration of small details (putting a wedge of lime into a bottle of Corona beer, for example), but it's never just about surface variables.

No matter how you measure it, in each case, Conversational Capital is about significant ("meaningful") change.

05.

CONVERSATIONAL CAPITAL
IS NOT BUZZ

Despite their many valuable insights, a lot of today's word-of-mouth and experiential marketers often operate under the wrong notions. They undertake what they do because they believe in generating "buzz," which they hope will get people talking. Some of these people will tell you that "there's no such thing as bad buzz," because any kind of talk draws attention to your product.

We believe, however, that this is a fundamental mistake and is an artifact of the outdated, mass-market paradigm. It assumes word-of-mouth and *experiential marketing* are directed toward the same goal as traditional 30-second television spots: generating awareness.

In his book *Experience the Message*, Max Lenderman demonstrates the shortcomings of this way of thinking.[7] He describes experiential marketing as "a situation in which consumers expect products, communications, and marketing campaigns to dazzle their senses, touch their hearts, and stimulate their minds." So far, we agree. However, when he goes on to write that "experiential marketing should enhance [the consumer's] experience with the brand and product *message* [our italics]," we find ourselves disagreeing. Again, as in the case in Chapter 4, "Why Conversational Capital Works," Max equates buzz, which is all surface, with word-of-mouth, which is about depth and continuity.

[7] Lenderman, Max. *Experience the Message.* New York: Carroll & Graf. 2006.

Putting pedometers into boxes of Special K or driving karaoke-equipped Jeeps into college campuses can certainly "enhance a brand and product message," but these activities do nothing to enhance the experiences of the products.

In our view, these efforts are ill fated, because, although simple awareness may get your product noticed, it won't necessarily encourage meaningful consumer interaction. As we have pointed out, meaningful interaction is what makes you a valuable subject of conversation.

How can you tell the difference between buzz and Conversational Capital?

- Buzz is often manufactured, and depends on media for its impact. Conversational Capital is embedded in the experience itself and relies on peer-to-peer conversations.

- Buzz is high impact, but it often has a short lifespan. Conversational Capital has legs because it is an identity shaper that has a meaningful and enduring place in the mind of consumers.

- Buzz is about getting attention at all costs. Conversational Capital is about meaning, integrity, and interaction.

CONVERSATIONAL CAPITAL MUST WALK THE WALK

Conversational Capital rests on a view of the consumer-experience dynamic that is nothing short of revolutionary. The traditional marketing paradigm is based on the notion of *communication*. Telling the right people about an experience often enough and under the right circumstances produces changes in consumer behavior. Conversational Capital, on the other hand, is about valuing *interaction*. It's about creating opportunities for meaningful interchange at every step along the experience continuum, from hearing about an experience, to sampling it, to taking it to heart and becoming an advocate.

This has a profound effect on the way we do business. We have enormous respect for great advertisers. And yet, they are fabulous storytellers who apply their formidable skills to an anti-quated paradigm. Advertising mogul Pat Fallon, for example, in his seminal piece "Juicing the Orange," writes about how Fallon Worldwide was built on creativity.[8] He and coauthor Fred Senn put it this way: "To us, the advertising industry was spending itself into irrelevance. We imagined a new kind of agency that would communicate with consumers in fresh, intelligent, and engaging ways, so that our consumers wouldn't have to shout ten times to be heard once."

In other words, Fallon and Senn call for high-saliency advertising. Naturally, we agree with this prescription, but we believe it's time to go a step further. We have to create highly salient campaigns for highly salient consumer experiences.

More creativity is not only laudable, but it's absolutely nec-essary. Fallon Worldwide has created some of the best and most memorable campaigns of the last decades. Yet, for all that, they are *advertising campaigns* that are still grounded in the notion of marshalling your best creative efforts to get a message across. We think that's not enough because it underestimates consumer motivation. Consumers no longer want just to be spoken to (or at), even if it entertains, amuses, and challenges them. *They want to be invited into a process of interaction and discovery.*

This paradigm shift has had an immediate impact on how marketing professionals try to generate word-of-mouth. Some are still stuck in the old way of doing things. Others understand that their efforts must be part of an ongoing conversation. John Moore, a former marketer for both Whole Foods and Starbucks (both great word-of-mouth successes), calls the former creators of *Creationist* word-of-mouth and the latter shapers of *Evolu-tionist* word-of-mouth.[9]

Creationist word-of-mouth, like traditional advertising and buzz, captures consumer attention through an artificially

[8] Fallon, Pat. *Juicing the Orange: How to Turn Creativity into a Powerful Business Advantage.* Boston, 2006.

[9] Moore, John. "Creationist WOM vs Evolutionist WOM." *Brand Autopsy.* April 17, 2006. <www.brandautopsy.com>.

amplified occurrence. Carl's Jr.'s Paris Hilton ads and Forehead Advertising for Golden Palace are good examples. Efforts like these draw attention, but note that they draw attention to the promotional occurrence itself, not the product being promoted (in other words, people talked more about Paris Hilton in a bikini and the guy with the tattoo on his face than they did about Carl's Jr. or Golden Palace).

Evolutionist word-of-mouth is about making the consumer experience better, turning consumers into evangelists. TIVO, Google, and Starbucks generated great and lasting word-of-mouth because, in each case, meaningful changes to the product or service created an experiential payoff. TIVO actually changes how you watch television. Google offers a better search engine, not better ads. Starbucks transforms buying a cup of coffee into a rarified opportunity to spoil yourself.

Simply put, Evolutionist word-of-mouth makes business a holistic phenomenon, and Conversational Capital is squarely in the Evolutionist's corner. That's why continuity and integrity are so important.

Continuity between who you say you are and who you *really* are is what makes an experience conductive. **Discontinuity** disappoints consumers, renders you vulnerable to criticism, and leads to negative word-of-mouth. In the world of Conversational Capital, integrity of experience is the name of the game.

The line between talking the talk and walking the walk was never the concern of traditional communications. As we've discussed, the context of a 30-second television spot or billboard doesn't leave much room for salience; you can hint at an experience, but you can't communicate it deeply. Conversational Capital is just the opposite; it works only by engaging consumers in high-saliency, rich experiences. Therefore, any discrepancy between what you promise and what you deliver can be fatal.

Does that sound like we're asking a lot of you? We don't think so, especially in light of the fact that the brands we admire deliver continuity and integrity without fail. Mac users can testify that Apple products are about freedom, great design, individuality, and innovation, down to the last experiential detail. method cleaning products not only look different, but they are different and they clean well. Red Bull isn't just a beverage; it is the key component of an intense lifestyle. adidas delivers on the promise of craftsmanship, performance, heritage, street credibility, and, increasingly, it delivers on a customized experience.

What about the opposite? We wanted to include Virgin as a great example of Conversational Capital in many sections of this book. We admire a lot about the brand, and we're in awe of Richard Branson's courage and independence of spirit. But a closer examination of the current reality of the brand experience told us we couldn't, which is too bad. In some ways, Virgin *is* a wonderful example of Conversational Capital. Richard Branson's story is a great founding myth: the maverick, daredevil entrepreneur who is dedicated to improving how things are done. Branson, through various stunts that include flying around the world in a hot air balloon and through forward-thinking initiatives (funding research into greener jet fuel) seems adept at generating positive word-of-mouth. Virgin Atlantic's Upper Class service, where flyers can stand together at a bar while in-flight, is a wonderful example of RSO. Virgin's visual signature, and Branson himself appear to have become iconic. By offering the best selection of pop culture books in its megastore book sections, Virgin gathers together members of the same international tribe.

The sticking problem is that Virgin doesn't quite measure up in terms of continuity. In recent years, Virgin has allowed a massive proliferation of substandard brands to emerge. These brands are so diffuse that it has become impossible to know what Virgin stands for now. Your experience as a user of Virgin Mobile is different from your experience as a flyer on Virgin Nigeria or from the experience of buying your dream wedding dress at Virgin Bride. It is hard to understand how many of these experiences are connected to one another, much less to the tribalism, icons, continuity, and RSO evoked.

Branson's the man and Virgin rocks; however, even Virgin could rock harder, couldn't it?

Some friends of ours recently returned from Zurich where they ate at a restaurant called The Blind Cow. The Blind Cow is run entirely by blind staff. Diners are led through thick curtains into a dining room that is completely dark. They arrive at their table, and various items are placed into their hands by staff at strategic points during the meal (here is your fork, here is your wine, and so on). Diners can only guess what they think the size of the room is or who else is there with them.

Sounds like great RSO, right? For the length of the meal, our friends could imagine what it was like to live as a blind person. As you would expect, they felt the rest of their senses sharpen the longer they were deprived of light. However, there was one problem. In such an environment, where our senses of touch, taste, and smell have become more discerning, we would hope that the experience of food and wine would be extraordinary. However, when asked, our friends said the food was "not so special." So, what could be conductive RSO becomes a stunt, albeit an interesting one. Unless you like eating in the dark, The Blind Cow may be something you try only once.

WE DIDN'T WRITE THIS BOOK FOR NUMBERS ON A CHART...

...or robots, or clothing store mannequins, or pet dogs and cats. We wrote it for human beings. We understand that reading is a holistic experience that should speak to real life, flesh-and-blood individuals who think and feel. Although the same conviction doesn't seem to drive traditional marketing frequently enough, it is how marketers should think of consumer experiences, too.

This is not to say that dogs and cats won't enjoy this book. They might, but just not in the same way.

SUMMING UP

- *The difference between Conversational Capital and buzz is the difference between noise and resonance. Buzz can happen through stunts that generate a lot of noise and attention, but it does nothing to ultimately change the nature of the consumer experience. It's shallow.*

- *Conversational Capital is resonant. It can emerge only when something significant has happened to the essence of the consumer experience. It can still lead to experiential efforts that are attention-getting, but these must be continuous and vibrate on the same wavelength with the consumer experience being marketed.*

QUESTIONS FOR DISCUSSION

Isn't Conversational Capital just another stunt?

What if you try to recreate your consumer experience by attempting to incorporate myth, by working to create an icon, or by appealing to a tribe? Isn't this just another glib attempt? We think the answer is no, because for any of those things to work, you must evoke something fundamental about your product or service. If it's just a matter of surface, you've failed. In addition, testing an effort for depth is the best way to separate a bombastic stunt from Conversational Capital.

06

CONVERSATIONAL CAPITAL
AND ADVOCACY

Just as Conversational Capital should not be mistaken for buzz, neither should it confused with advocacy.

Advocacy—the vocal support of consumers to their peers—is an excellent thing. That's what word-of-mouth success does. As we discussed in Chapter 5, "Conversational Capital Is Not Buzz," advocacy is the most authoritative form of marketing communication because it is sincere and generally unsolicited.

The key difference between advocacy and Conversational Capital is one of degree. What we've observed about Conversational Capital is that it raises the stakes of advocacy even higher. Conversational Capital doesn't just create advocates. In many cases, it creates *converts*.

True Cirque du Soleil fans are *fans* in every sense. There are true believers who are fanatical in their devotion to the shows. Furniture outlets offer discounted, stylish products for the home, but none has become what IKEA has—not just a store, but an integrated part of the modern lifestyle. Schwartz's Delicatessen isn't the only place in Montréal where you can buy a smoked meat sandwich, but it is the only one where customers line up in a snowstorm to eat. In each of these cases, the experience has become part of how consumers live and breathe.

One can advocate for experiences that mean less. For example, if someone asks you for advice on what automobile he should buy, you might endorse one over another based on price, style, and underlying consumer need. If you need to give a hotel or restaurant recommendation, you probably won't hesitate to suggest a place that won't disappoint, but you may not offer much more information. In either case, you will have endorsed a product to a peer, but ultimately, there may be little significance in the endorsement. The endorsement may be nothing more than a simple social transaction.

Conversational Capital occurs when consumer experiences become a key lifestyle component. In such cases, advocacy—speaking out for the product—may not even be necessary. Instead, the experience may have become so much a part of how one lives that talk about it becomes like talk about the weather, one's home, or how one slept last night. That level of significance speaks for itself. In its own quiet way, it's more resonant than advocacy could ever be.

SUMMING UP

Conversational Capital and advocacy should not be confused for one another. Conversational Capital raises the stakes of advocacy even higher, by creating true converts or fans.

07

CONVERSATIONAL CAPITAL
IS FOR EVERYONE

Reading through our observations so far, the question might arise: "Is Conversational Capital for everyone?" The answer is yes. It might work for high-end, live entertainment, or certain retailers, but what if you work for a packaged goods company or a discount airline?

It *is* true that premium, experience-rich products and services lend themselves well to Conversational Capital. This is only natural. They are targeted to sophisticated consumers who are exacting and who demand innovation, differentiation, and customization. These consumers, in turn, reward companies that take risks. As you read through this book, however, it will become clear that Conversational Capital is observable through a complete range of consumer experiences, not just high margin products and services.

For now, though, consider a few examples:

- Remember Tang? The experience of consuming these humble flavored drink crystals became enriched by myth when it became known that the product was used by members of the Apollo space mission astronauts. Suddenly, you weren't just drinking a flavored drink anymore; you were sharing in the Space Age experience.

- Guinness and Corona are two examples of commodity products (beer) that stand out because of the presence of Conversational Capital. Guinness is dark and, unlike other beers, is best enjoyed at room temperature (RSO with a soupçon of ritual). Corona is the beer you drink with a lime—another opportunity to partake of a blend of ritual and RSO.

- Altoids can be found in any candy store, yet they became hip and talked about despite its mass production. Is it any accident that we can spot many engines of Conversational Capital in this humble mint? The unique metallic packaging is a form of RSO. These days, we expect our candy to be wrapped in foil and paper, not packed in a tin box. Altoids deliberately harkens back to a forgotten brand history, to a time when candy was somehow more authentic (myth). Lastly, the jingling sound of candy in a tin, seeing your reflection on the bottom side of the lid when you open the box, and hearing the satisfying snap as it closes—these have an aspect of ritual.

- Crocs up-ended some fundamental notions about style and aesthetic appeal, yet these all-purpose, relatively inexpensive shoes and sandals have enjoyed tremendous success by leveraging the power of RSO (they look and feel different from anything else), tribalism (you are or are not a person who wears Crocs), and EPO (unlike other sandals, they come in a range of colors, so you can choose what suits you best).

- Kangol caps became fashionable for a time through a simple trick of RSO—you could wear the hat backwards. Those who "got it" became members of the same tribe.

- When does a notebook stop being just a notebook? When it is a Moleskine. Hemingway wrote his novels in Moleskine notebooks. Picasso sketched in them (myth). The notebook has often been recognized for its distinctive shape, coated paper, and iconic elastic band (RSO). In a digital age, this seeming analog anachronism has rediscovered its place among the creative class (tribalism).

Finally, consider the case of Robin Hood Flour. Robin Hood is cited in university-level marketing courses as a case where a commodity was turned into a powerful brand. The reality is that flour is flour. Although it may come in different packages, flour has the same properties and serves the same use, no matter who sells it. Yet, baking aficionados swear by Robin Hood and consider it superior to any other flour. The makers of Robin Hood were able to do this by intuitively and organically applying the principles of Conversational Capital to their product. First, they recognized that bakers are a tribe with their own set of expectations and needs. By offering recipes and organizing bake-offs, they helped to enable and maintain the formation of this tribe. Secondly, they have never changed their distinctive yellow packaging, sporting a simple drawing of an Errol Flynn-esque Robin Hood in profile. The packaging stands out on the grocery shelf and provides an example of RSO. Aware of the reputation they established, the makers of Robin Hood have ardently maintained their standards and approach in the face of changing fashions. So, bakers always feel secure in recommending Robin Hood.

Come to think of it, another fine example of Conversational Capital is the least expensive item we could think of: Bazooka Joe bubblegum. Bazooka Joe and his cartoon pals are icons of a simpler, more free-wheeling childhood. Because they are packaged in single pieces, they are an example of RSO. Reading and collecting the comics that came with Bazooka Joe bubblegum felt like a ritual.

You see the point. However, to hammer it home, we'd like to remind our readers that, in the world of consumption, everything is an *experience*. We may not consider cleaning toilets or waiting in line hallmark *moments*, but they are *experiential* activities nonetheless. They can be improved and made more memorable and significant. Making this investment ensures they are not only remembered, but that they will become the subject of conversation.

This should be obvious. However, many traditional market-ers seem to have missed the point entirely. James Allen, head of Bain & Company's global strategy practice, put it best when he wrote: "Customers ... want customer experiences, not just pro-ducts. And they are not impressed by most of what is currently on offer. When Bain & Company recently surveyed executives of 362 firms, we found that 80 percent believed they delivered a 'superior experience' to their customers. When we asked cus-tomers, however, they told a very different story: They said only 8 percent of companies were really delivering."[10]

Why this schism between marketer and consumer percep-tion? Because too many marketers are still hamstrung by the mass-marketing paradigm. They still perceive brand experien-ces as being limited to print campaigns and 30-second television and radio spots. They don't understand that achieving customer satisfaction is not the same thing as creating a meaningful expe-rience. Customer satisfaction is a mere "*green fee*;" it is the price of entry into any category. A meaningful experience does more; it provides consumers identity-shaping residual value and can turn them into brand ambassadors. However, too many marke-ters have failed to assert that every *touchpoint* is an opportunity to create such an experience.

In a *Harvard Business Review* piece titled "Understanding Customer Experience," Christopher Meyer and André Schwa-ger explain this clearly when they write: "The result is that there is too often a split between what marketing promises and the brand. 'Customer experience' encompasses every aspect of a company's offering—the quality of customer care, of course, but also advertising, packaging, product and service features, ease of use, and reliability."[11]

[10] Allen, J., Reicheld, F., Hamilton, B. and Markey, R. "Closing the Delivery Gap." *Bain & Company*. London. October 5, 2005.

[11] Meyer, C. and Schwager, A. "Understanding Customer Experience." *Harvard Business Review*. Cambridge, MA. February 1, 2007.

We think experiences are even more than that, ranging from social responsibility to retail, from seeding to experiential marketing.

Conversational Capital seeks to repair that disconnect. The engines of Conversational Capital can all be understood as "experience enhancers." That's why they work as effectively as they do, which is why we examine them in greater detail.

To reiterate, these are:

1. Rituals

2. Exclusive Product Offering (EPO)

3. Myths

4. Relevant Sensory Oddity (RSO)

5. Icons

6. Tribalism

7. Endorsement

8. Continuity

Let's examine each of them in more detail.

SUMMING UP

While Conversational Capital certainly sings in high-margin, experience-rich categories, it can be discerned across the consumer goods spectrum—from commodity foods to notebooks to disposable footwear. Examine products and services for the presence of the Eight Engines, and you'll spot the ones we mean.

QUESTIONS FOR DISCUSSION

Can bubblegum be a significant, integrated lifestyle product?

We've been making a lot of claims for Conversational Capital, particularly that it creates consumer experiences that are resonant and meaningful. Can it really apply to a bubblegum manufacturer? In the case of Bazooka Joe, we think it does because—by design or sheer luck—it is the one bubblegum that has become an icon of carefree childhood for so many (and what is more bathed in meaning and intensity than childhood memories?).

When you learn how to detect its presence, Conversational Capital is everywhere. We look forward to receiving some examples from you.

PART TWO

THE ENGINES OF CONVERSATIONAL CAPITAL

08.

RITUALS

Rituals are as old as human society. The earliest known cave paintings date back some 32,000 years and were found in Chauvet, France. These highly sophisticated paintings of animals are thought to have served a ritual purpose—by coming together to create and later view the paintings, the tribe was reminded of their special relationship with the animals they hunted and to one another.

Recent evidence shows that rituals might even predate *Homo Sapiens*. The Neanderthals, our sentient cousins, are known to have had rituals of their own. They buried their dead and made art—a 35,000 year-old artifact fashioned by Neanderthals was discovered in 2003. Perhaps unsurprisingly, it is a crude mask, a rough Neanderthal face.

Our propensity for ritual may be encoded in our DNA. It is passed down from generation to generation, essential to the process of socialization. We use rituals to mark events and relationships as significant and, at times, sacred. We ritualize fertility, birth, coming-of-age, marriage, and death, elevating them to special status. By sharing rituals together, we bond socially, too.

In other words, rituals are important to identity formation for both individuals and groups. Identity formation is the bedrock of storytelling: "Who am I? Where am I going? Who is like me or not like me? Why am I here?"

Some existentially loaded theories suggest that we enact rituals as a defense against the fundamentally arbitrary and chaotic nature of the universe. Whether or not this is universally true, it does seem to motivate certain superstitious personal rituals. These are the idiosyncratic gestures and habits people use to ward off stress and pressure. Baseball players demand certain songs before they come to bat; other athletes ritually tie their shoes a certain way, artists arrange their materials just so, motorists stick to certain "lucky" parking places, and so on Almost everybody has such rituals. They work for us because, most of the time, we find them comforting. The more comforting they are, the more often we come back to them. Perhaps this is because they remind us of who we are and where we belong.

Whatever the real reason for rituals, they are undoubtedly a powerful force in human culture. Conversational Capital suggests that when rituals become part of your experience, it makes them more memorable and worthy of conversation.

But how do you integrate rituals into your product design and marketing? This is tricky because most rituals happen organically and over time. They aren't typically manufactured from the top down. Instead, they are user-generated. Trying too hard to create rituals can make them seem forced and odd. Instead, smart manufacturers and marketers put elements in place to allow the process to happen and then build on it.

It's important to remember that *rituals* are not the same as *habits*. Both are repeated forms of behavior, but rituals are of a higher order because we use them to designate certain experiences as special.

Remember, too, that rituals are to some degree supposed to be comforting. They are most effective when unchanged over time—because of this, they should be thought of as an element in the experience mix that improves consistency.

As we said, it's tricky, but not impossible. Many consumer experiences are already highly ritualized:

- At restaurants, we are greeted by hosts and waited on in a stylized manner that has become so ingrained in global culture that we don't even think about it. The same is true at hotels, where we invariably follow the same steps:

check in, walk to room with or without bell person, slide card in lock, and so on.

- Many nightclubs are also places of ritual, particularly in the lineup before entry. The lineup naturally creates a sense of procession, and clubs would do well to build on this. In lineups, nightclub goers become part of a community where they are vying for position and recognition. There is an underlying sense of tension: "Will I be among the select few who make it in?" Those who can skip the lineup altogether are the high priests and priestesses of the club scene.

- Shopping for clothes has also become standardized and ritualized. As in restaurants, we are waited on and made to feel special. We enter the hushed, private confines of the changing room like a confessional. After we are inside, we take stock of ourselves and confront our best and worst qualities. We hope that we will come out of the booth improved and regenerated.

Rituals are comforting, but too much comfort robs rituals of their power. We have observed that in already ritual-rich industries, the power of rituals to shape memorable experiences has diminished over time. Through widespread use over decades, ritual has sunk past comfort to mere banality. Nevertheless, some companies have reinvested the same rituals with new power by slightly altering them and giving them a new face. Following are some examples:

- Skylofts at MGM Grand in Las Vegas is a super-premium hotel offering penthouse apartments at $1,000 a night and up. Every detail has been arranged to make Skylofts guests feel they are a cut above the rest. More importantly, in terms of Conversational Capital, they have tweaked greeting rituals to make guests feel that way as soon as they arrive in Las Vegas. Each Skylofts guest is whisked from the airport to the hotel in a chauffeur-driven Maybach.

Anyone can travel to the hotel in a stretch limousine in Vegas. But only Skyloft guests travel by Maybach.

- When a bride-to-be and her fiancé go to Tiffany to resize her ring, they might be greeted with champagne and chocolate. This ritualized coddling fosters a formidable bond with the buyer, making the clients feel cherished.

- On Singapore Airlines' premium class services, Singapore girls bow to you as you enter the plane. When you take your seat, they bring you a signature cocktail and pajamas and take your meal order.

- At Pat's Cheese Steaks in Philadelphia, you must order correctly or be sent to the back of the line. If you ask for anything other than Cheese Whiz, you're yelled at. Onions can be added only if you say "Wid," or left out if you say, "Widdout."

- Bape is an international clothing retailer from Asia that is currently making inroads across North America. When a customer wants to try on an item of clothing, he is handed an item of clothing of the same size and cut but not the original item! While it may seem strange at first, this slight change in ritual makes the original item of clothing seem more valuable. When the customer leaves with the original item, he can do so assured of the knowledge that no one else on earth has worn that particular shirt or pair of pants, and so on. Once again, a slight change in accepted ritual makes the client feel special.

- For many readers, buying and reading the Sunday *New York Times* has become an important ritual. Paging through the Bible-thick newspaper, one feels the act filled with importance and significance. Time is suspended as the reader confronts the forces that shape our individual and collective destinies.

- Tupperware distinguished itself from the competition by transforming the buying process into a social ritual: the Tupperware Party.

- One doesn't just buy a box of Tic Tacs and start eating them. More often than not, they are consumed with a ritual first: the percussive shake of the package.

- A beloved episode of *Seinfeld* ("The Soup Nazi") revolves around the dictates and strictures of a New York City soup vendor. The real-life "Soup Nazi" who inspired the episode became known for the strict and somewhat arcane rules to be observed when ordering. Those customers who were able to figure out these rules without incurring his wrath were able to feel they had somehow "made it." Less confrontational, but still memorable, are the scores of Chinese restaurants across North America where there is almost no ordering ritual. Rather than actually speak to the waiter, customers write down their orders and hand them over.

Ritualized behavior is well rooted in the service and clothing industries, but they don't have to be limited to them. Some packaged goods lend themselves well to rituals, too. We previously cited Corona beer, which drinkers invariably consume with the ritual addition of lime. Oreo cookies can be said to have become ritualized as well: Many consumers remove one of the chocolate wafers to eat the cream filling first.

READ THIS BOOK UPSIDE DOWN...

...or wearing swimming goggles, or while swishing the air with a feather duster. By slightly changing a mundane activity, you just might give it ritual power. Remember that episode of Seinfeld *where George started eating candy bars with a knife and fork, and every one started imitating him? People love new rituals. So be careful what you do; it just might catch on.*
   (Ah, Seinfeld.*)*

Examples abound. Some people leave the aluminum seal of the peanut butter jar in place after it is opened. Others dig into their ice cream from the exact center of the container. Still, others wash from top to bottom in the shower, or from bottom to top. How to properly place toilet paper—top out or bottom out—is a debate that raged through Ann Lander's syndicated newspaper advice column for years.

In light of this deeply ingrained tendency, smart product design and marketing should take into account the ritualistic potential of even the most common items. Can you do something to make the item in question more ritualized?

SUMMING UP

Rituals are behaviors or rites we engage in to mark certain activities as exalted. When ritual behavior becomes associated with a consumer experience, it is marked out as more resonant.

QUESTIONS FOR DISCUSSION

Can you spot a new ritual?

We recently ate at a restaurant in Tucson where ordering from the menu was done away with altogether. In this place, you ate what the maverick chef decided to prepare that night. It was an interesting twist on an expected consumer ritual. (And the food paid off the promise of uniqueness and special attention, too.)

Have you noticed any new inversions or revolutions in how a product or service is supposed to be consumed? How did it make you feel? Care to share it with us?

09.

INITIATION

Although we perceive it as a subset of Ritual, Initiation is a Conversational Capital engine with a power all its own. Important passages in life are often marked by initiation of one kind or another. Significantly, these initiation rituals always involve some discomfort, if not outright pain.

It may sound odd in a book about experience design and marketing to talk about pain and discomfort. After all, most producers and marketers in a consumer society would tell you that their only goal is to please. Consumption is supposed to provide us a way out of discomfort. It's supposed to be about pleasure.

Yet salient experiences, the cornerstone of Conversational Capital, would not be interesting without a minimal amount of unpleasantness built in. Unpleasantness is the stuff of dramatic tension. In his journey, the hero must engage in conflict and overcome hurdles and obstacles to triumph. Sometimes, these conflicts and hurdles are external. Sometimes they are internal. In either case, without conflict, there would be no story.

Take a moment and think about the stories you hear. How many of them involve someone overcoming hardship to get to a worthwhile, shareable experience?

Someone will tell you they almost died getting to the top of Everest. Another will tell you how much trouble it was to find this exceptionally good Hong Kong film they just saw—they had to go to a special store in New York City, and almost got lost getting there! In the days before Internet sales, people would tell you how long they stood in line to get a ticket for a concert. Some will talk about how long they waited outside in the pouring rain outside a hotel just to meet a celebrity. Still, another will go on about how hard it was to figure out the intricacies of a favorite game or book. The world of amateur athletics and extreme sports—from triathlons to bungee jumping—is filled with challenges and hurdles overcome (pun intended).

There often seems to be a direct correlation between the quality and memorability of an experience and the work it took to fulfill that experience in the first place. The ability to have weathered the storm is what separates the initiated few from the uninitiated. Initiation, then, is a key engine that makes consumers feel they are part of a select group of special people—because they have *earned* it.

How do you make that feeling part of your experience without alienating consumers? Our society is geared toward ease-of-use and rapid fulfillment. Make things too complicated or delay gratification too long, and you'll still get people to talk about you. It's just that the things they say won't be so nice. The opposite is true, too: If you make things too easy or pander too much, you'll lose the interest of sophisticated consumers who are most likely to spread the word about a good experience.

The truth is that people like to be challenged. They just don't want to be challenged *too much*. Most initiation rituals from real life (adult circumcision, frat party hazing) clearly fall under the "too much" banner. Incorporating rituals into consumption experiences requires a lighter, more discerning touch.

Remember what we said about Cirque? As we mentioned earlier, performers at each Cirque du Soleil show lead the audience through a gentle form of initiation. It works well, but few products and experiences are circus- or clown-based. So what can we learn about Cirque du Soleil's use of initiation that can be applied to other aspects of consumer experience?

One valuable observation is that Cirque du Soleil has turned an unavoidable logistical problem into an engine of Conversational Capital. How so? Reality dictates that before a show begins, audiences must of necessity take the time to find their seats and fill the theater. Each audience member is on his own schedule, so naturally not everybody will arrive at the same time. Pre-show clowning allows that "dead time" to be filled in creatively and to be turned into an opportunity for gentle initiation. Initiation through clowning erases the boredom, judo flips slight discomfort to its advantage, and turns possible downtime into an opportunity for an enriched experience.

What aspect of your business might be transformed in this way? In the hospitality industry, lineups can be inevitable. At hotel check-ins and in restaurants, getting the service you want can take some time and be an unavoidable irritant. These industries can transform irritants into initiation by slightly rethinking certain practices.

This is what happened, organically, at Schwartz's in Montréal. The almost inevitable outdoor lineup has become a rite of passage to be enjoyed. Schwartz's would be crazy to, say, expand the restaurant inside or provide for greater comfort outside. Clients expect the lineup. It is a mark of Schwartz's quality, elevating it to almost mythic proportions. The smoked meat seems tastier and the small confines of the restaurant feel all the warmer because of it.

The same dynamic occurs at Hakkasan, a premium dining establishment located in a basement on London's Hanway Place. In order to get into the restaurant in the first place, diners must enter through a back alley. At first blush, one would think that locating a four-star establishment in such a place would be counter-intuitive. And yet, it has become a much repeated part of the Hakkasan story. In fact, it's become an often imitated, worldwide phenomenon, stretching to New York, Buenos Aires, Paris, and Tokyo. The inevitable passage from street to restaurant has become a challenge one is proud to have overcome. By getting over the *ewww* factor, the consumer proves that he "gets it;" the consumer is past such preconceived notions and, is therefore, *initiated*.

Theme parks have become expert at turning waiting time into possibilities for initiation. Waiting in line for rides is inevitable. It has become commonplace to extend the experience of certain theme park attractions outward into the waiting line. As one gets closer to the action, one usually enters a dark, enclosed place where characters and themes from the attraction are used to create tension and drama. When you arrive at the ride with your children in tow, the end result is that you feel you have been initiated in some way into the experience. But a warning is in order: The experience is ubiquitous and common across almost all major theme-park attractions. Ubiquity and commonality are Conversational Capital killers. When something becomes too run-of-the-mill, you don't feel compelled to talk about it anymore. Enriching an experience with *Relevant Sensory Oddity* (RSO) can help.

The lineup at bars is another area ripe for transformation into initiation. What people most remember about bars—what renders the experience of one different from another—are two things: the lineup and the bathrooms. The rest of the nightclub experience is typically too diffuse to be that memorable. The lineups are a natural rite of initiation, as mentioned in a previous chapter. We either make it in and are part of the elect, or we don't. Exploring ways to make the process more memorable and more meaningful is highly recommended. Can the bar experience be extended outward, as is the case with theme park attractions?

Sometimes, the simple addition of an interesting architectural detail can help augment the guest's sense of initiation. In the case of three-dimensional consumption experiences like hotels, bars, restaurants, theme parks, casinos, and even public buildings like museums and libraries, the transition from the "outside world" to the experience itself should be taken into special consideration. Creating a tube-like corridor into the experience, for example, can heighten the sense of transition from banal to exceptional. If the tube or passageway is made more dramatic through sound or lighting effects, it can discomfit visitors in a positive way and heighten dramatic tension. Simply walking through such a passageway can feel like a form of initiation. Stairs, ramps, or simple wall projections can serve the same function as a tube.

Can such thinking be applied to consumer products? Some marketers might resign themselves to the thought that you can't create the same effect with packaged goods, but the truth of the matter is that smart marketers have engineered stimulation into the act of buying a product or opening its package. Figure out the packaging and you have become *initiated* into something new and slightly revolutionary.

There are also signs and signifiers to be used in packaging and selling products that can challenge and stimulate users. Decode these signs and signifiers, and you are an initiate. Consider the following examples:

- Buy an item from IKEA, and there's initiation built right in. First, you have to decode IKEA'S language and learn to distinguish a Jerkker from a Lesvik or a Minnen. Then, you have to pass the "waiting-in-the-warehouse" test. Finally, IKEA forces you to unpack components and build your own furniture—the final step in your initiation as an IKEA customer.

- Apple has made opening its packaging feel like a religious experience while reducing packaging material by a third. An exercise in elegance and minimalism, it resonates with Zen simplicity and augments the emotional intensity of opening a product package.

- UPS envelopes are sealed with string. It's a small gesture, but tearing the string makes the experience of opening the package more formal, important, and fulfilling.

Finally, some of the best products naturally invite initiation. People who drive sports cars are often highly familiar with the mechanical complexities of their vehicles. To drive a Porsche, in other words, it often helps to have challenged yourself and done the homework, so you can speak about the experience convincingly. PC power users pride themselves in their abilities to solve technical and programming challenges.

A new type of espresso machine has entered the market. It offers users a disposable "pod" system; simply insert your pod into the machine, and it will make a perfect espresso for you.

Efficient, yes, but this Johnny-come-lately robs coffee aficiona-dos of the feeling of accomplishment associated with learning how to use conventional espresso-making machines in the first place. As true initiates, amateur baristas look down their noses at naive pod users.

- Garrett's Popcorn on North Michigan avenue in Chicago and the Louis Vuitton flagship store on the Champs-Elysées in Paris couldn't be more different. And yet each of them challenges consumers to wait in a long lineup before entering the store, offering excellent examples of initiation. The longer you wait, the more special the inside of the store will feel.

- Donut lovers become initiates at Lee's Doughnuts at the Granville Island Public Market in Vancouver. Insiders know exactly when the warm Honey Dip donuts are coming out, so only they—and not the latecomers—get to participate in the delicious ritual of eating the donuts at just the right time.

WE COULD HAVE SET THIS BOOK IN DINGBATS

✢◆▼ ▼✳◐▼ ▶□◆●✳ □□□◐❀◆●❖l ✳□✳◆❖ l□◆ ✳□◐ll!!!!

Initiation is about making an experience more chal-lenging, and therefore more meaningful. Setting the last chapter in Dingbats would have been challenging, alright, but it wouldn't have been smart. Putting people off balance and then rewarding them for their discom-fort is good. Making them too uncomfortable without a decent payoff is annoying.

To figure out what the previous line says, you could try to copy and paste it after...no, forget it. It says, "But that would probably drive you crazy!"

SUMMING UP

Initiation is a special subset of ritual. When consumers feel they have worked a little harder to acquire special knowledge of or access to a consumer experience, they feel set apart.

QUESTIONS FOR DISCUSSION

Can you push people too far?

Our first instinct is to say that initiation works best when it doesn't make consumers feel too uncomfortable. Lineups are one thing if they pay off—such as a gorgeous Louis Vuitton store. It's quite another if it's simply the result of entrenched bad management (recall the last time you boarded a plane).

And yet, some consumer experiences really do push the discomfort envelope. You can now pay to experience zero gravity by nose diving in a plane at terrifying speed. Or, you can ride a makeshift flying machine off a 30-foot pier into icy water at a Red Bull Flügtag event. Neither is everyone's cup of tea, and yet they attract certain consumers who rave about the experience.

Where do you stand on that question?

10.

EXCLUSIVE PRODUCT OFFERING (EPO)

Over six billion people live on the planet today. That is more than have lived throughout human history up to now. In other words, we, the living, outnumber all of history's dead. With so many people around, can anyone be truly unique?

The explosive growth of customization in recent years tells us the answer is a loud, resounding "yes." Consumers demand customization and differentiation. Given the chance to take advantage of these, no two people express themselves in the same way.

It's no wonder: our desire to be one-of-a-kind is deeply seated—and it reflects reality. None of us looks exactly the same or is built the same way. Each of us has individual rhythms, habits, tastes, and preferences. The differences between us might be subtle, but they are present nonetheless.

Decades of mass production and mass marketing might have temporarily blinded us to this essential truth. Across the consumer spectrum, we still struggle with experiences tailored to the least common denominator. To please everybody, these experiences have been robbed of flavor and richness. Their stickiness and memorability have been neutralized. How many hamburgers can you eat before they all begin to taste the same? How many uncomfortable coach class commuter flights can you endure before they blend into one dull blur? How many suburban houses in similarly faceless North American communities can you visit before you forget where you are and why you bothered to get out of bed in the first place?

Exclusive product offering (EPO) should not be confused with the notion of the Unique Selling Proposition (USP) proposed by Rosser Reeves. USP is what distinguishes one product from another, for example, "good, consistent coffee." The problem is that many USPs turn out to be not so unique on close examination. Any number of coffee retailers can promise "good, consistent coffee."

Rather, EPO is about experiences that stand out because they remind us we are individuals. Often, EPO is driven by customization. The shorthand is this: The more an experience belongs to me and me alone, the more powerful it will be—and the more inclined I will be to talk about it.

Examples abound:

- Starbucks is a huge, mainstream phenomenon. On the surface, you might mistakenly think that it's a glaring example of homogeneity. Like so many others, it offers a variation on "good, consistent coffee." Yet it provides a leading example of mass customization and, therefore, EPO. Stand in line at a Starbucks, and you notice that few customers order the same thing. The nonfat caramel-nonfat-soy-macchiato is just one of the dizzying array of blended coffee beverages that have become part of our cultural fabric. Each is made for you, on the spot—a completely exclusive product that only you will taste.

  Any expert in operational efficiency would be of the advice that standardizing the tailor-made fabrication of Starbucks coffee would result in an increase in productivity and profitability. We hold the contrary opinion. We believe that doing so would rob Starbucks of one of its most powerful engines of Conversational Capital.

- Shopping the iTunes Music Store turns the consumption of music into an EPO hallmark. Because you have the freedom to buy separate tracks rather than entire CDs, you create your own experience of an artist's music. iTunes software enables you to collect that music in a highly personalized library that is like no other.

- Car owners used to express themselves through their choice of vehicles. The MINI Cooper takes that ideal further by enabling the vehicle itself to become a canvas for self-expression. BMW claims that no two MINIs are the same. Buyers custom-configure their MINIs down to the paint-scheme on the roof and hood.

- The Toyota Scion takes customization further by providing tools and advice on how to personalize its cars down to the minutest details, with more than 40 different aftermarket accessories. Scion is at the forefront of a trend that appeals to teens and young adults called "tuning"—a practice frowned upon by competitors like Honda, which warn that tuning can void the warranty.

- Jones Soda is an independent beverage producer bottling an array of unusual flavors packaged in clear bottles that bear the faces of its most passionate customers. It invites consumers into the product design process. Jones Soda drinkers are asked to participate in the creation of new packaging, new labels, even new flavors. The next special edition Jones Soda product can be yours in every sense of the word.

- Some retailers answer our need for exclusive product offering by enabling customers to create highly tailored products. The *mi originals*, offered at adidas-owned Originals outlets are a case in point. Customers can have shoes tailored to fit their feet exactly in limited-edition patterns and styles. The shoes are inscribed with the name of the wearer. Bertrand has a pair—one of only 75 pairs of shoes in the world that look like his and the only pair custom-fit to his feet and inscribed with his name. The shoes can be provided only at adidas stores, adding to the richness of the retail experience.

- Harley Davidson has been embraced in a way that no other motorcycle manufacturer has. This has occurred, in part, because Harleys are highly customizable. Own a Harley, and chances are that yours is like no other rider's.

- Even without offering explicitly customized products, retailers can enhance the sense of exclusivity in their stores. The Spanish retailer Zara is an excellent case in point. Zara offers the most up-to-date selection of current trends of any competing clothing retailer. They do this by changing their selection of merchandise every two weeks in virtually immediate response to emergent couture and street trends. This contrasts sharply with brands like The Gap that refresh their merchandise only on a quarterly basis.

- The Nordstrom shopping experience has always been about intense personalization and interaction. It's not about off-the-shelf purchases—it's about custom combinations that increase the quality of your shopping experience. This is a store where employees are empowered to help you in any department, not just "their section." So they can help you look great when you walk out of the store.

- Even the humble Cracker Jack box provides a form of EPO. Because the prize in each box is different, your experience is never quite the same as anyone else's. Kinder Eggs offer a similar experience.

High-end experiences take customization even further still:

- The Regent Hotel in Hong Kong surprises first-time diners by presenting them with personalized, monogrammed napkins. And from doormen to housekeeping, staff just seem to know your name.

- Vertu is an independently run subsidiary of Nokia that handcrafts luxury mobile handsets to individual specifications. If you want a diamond-encrusted, 24-carat, gold-encased phone, it can make one for you. Just don't leave it lying around at the V.I.P. party.

- The Neiman Marcus Christmas catalog offers the high-end buyer extremely limited-edition experiences, such as week-long vacations on Richard Branson's Necker Island, original art, and golf lessons with Arnold Palmer. For those who can afford them and for those who dare to dream, these exclusive experiences create fodder for stories that are sure to keep the Neiman Marcus name on people's lips. At a time when department stores are doing everything they can to emulate discounters, Neiman Marcus is cementing its place as the house of vogue.

Although EPO sings in high-end experiences, it is important to remember that the draw of exclusivity extends to all social strata. Human behavior experts began to notice this as far back as the 1930s when they described "The Hawthorne Effect."

In the 1930s, a team of researchers from Harvard Business School were commissioned to carry out employee research at a Western Electric (now Lucent Technologies) production plant in Hawthorne, near Chicago. The researchers invited a small group of participants out of the general workforce to test new working conditions. They were surprised to discover that the small group's productivity increased with exposure to these new conditions—even in directly contradictory situations. Working under stronger light resulted in increased productivity. But then, so did working under increasingly dimmer lighting conditions. Working shorter hours had the same effect as working longer hours.

The team of researchers soon realized that increases in productivity had nothing to do with trial conditions—*and everything to do with being singled out to participate in the trial in the first place.* Being part of the research made the individuals in the trial group feel valued, special, and important. The crucial link to word-of-mouth was this: The researchers saw that receiving ego gratification created a positive emotional bond to what was trialed. Research participants became ambassadors for the trial conditions. A series of further trials showed this result to be more or less systematic, and the term "The Hawthorne Effect" was coined to describe it.

Psychologically, the truth of the Hawthorne Effect seems evident. If you want something from people, it's always a good idea to ask them for advice. By soliciting their opinion, you create goodwill and flatter their ego, and they feel indebted to you.

EPO works because it leverages the Hawthorne Effect by empowering consumers to become agents of co-creation in the experience. That feeling of having taken part in the creation of an experience generates favorable advocacy. Need some examples of consumer-driven empowerment in action? Think of American Idol, Crayola (which invites users to name new colors), and Build-a-Bear (where customers create their own teddy bears), to name but a few.

Outside of customizing an experience, is there some other way you can harness the power of EPO? The answer is to remember that EPO makes *experiences* feel exclusive. Conversational Capital encourages us to focus on the quality of consumption experiences. You can customize all you want, but if the customization you offer is experientially deadpan, it is less likely to be sticky.

Remember what we said about iTunes? iTunes is just one example of the customization that is a cornerstone of online consumption. Google enables users to create their searches, their way, because of tools such as Google Mobile. Unlike offline bookstores, Amazon has no restriction to the number of books it can offer users. By using data-warehousing and neural networks, Amazon builds a profile of the preferences of each customer and compares that to those of customers who purchased similar merchandise. The result is a list of recommendations that, more often than not, reflects your tastes and interests and is like no other user's.

YOU'RE THINKING ABOUT EATING
A DONUT RIGHT NOW

Or maybe not.

When it comes to exclusive product offering, books might not provide the best example. After all, this book should be the same for anyone who reads it. We could make it feel more exclusive if we were somehow able to reach out from its pages and remind you that you are unique and unlike any other reader. We could mention your name, for instance. (SAY YOUR NAME OUT LOUD HERE.) Or, we could read your mind.

Are you sure you couldn't go for a donut right now, (YOUR NAME HERE)?

SUMMING UP

EPO occurs when a consumer experience offers a notable degree of individualization. When you feel something has been designed just for you, or in a distinctly personal way, you can claim an experience as your own, it becomes more salient. EPO sings in high-end experiences, but we've also observed it in simple products such as Cracker Jack or the Kinder Egg.

QUESTIONS FOR DISCUSSION

Doesn't letting go of standardization invite chaos?

The Mass Marketing Age was built on **standardization** and uniformity. One-size-fits-all was supposed to be good for everyone. It certainly made production easier. Customization poses a real challenge for those who see it as, at best, frankly too much bother, or, at worst, a threat to the social order.

This, however, is archaic thinking. Look around you; you can see increasing diversity and ever more specifically targeted segmentation. EPO isn't a challenge—it's a more true reflection of human diversity. That's why it works.

Do you have a valid argument in favor of more standardization and less customization? We'd love to hear it.

Isn't EPO just customization?

Not at all—because customization can so often be a surface variable that in no way alters the resonance of an experience. Form letters and e-mails are "customized" to a certain degree, but we sense that they are in no way meaningfully tailored to the individual receiving them. Further, some experiences that are rendered more salient by EPO are not actually "customized" in the classic sense. For example, no one has designed a Kinder Egg specifically for you—yet because there are enough variants on the market, yours will still feel special when you buy it.

11.

OVER-DELIVERY

Exclusive product offering (EPO) doesn't necessarily have to do with customization. Often, an experience can stand out as unique through a phenomenon we call *over-delivery*.

Think about the people you've met in your lifetime or the experiences you've lived. Which of them do you remember most? Which have you been most likely to talk about? Do any of them stand out because they were just "good enough" or because they were sublime in their mediocrity?

Probably not. We remember things and talk about them because they are distinctly intense and meaningful. They were funnier, more exciting, more poetic, more terrifying, and so on. In other words, they over-delivered on one or more aspects of human experience.

The goal of Conversational Capital is to create experience differentiation. The residual value of a product or service is increased when consumers are satisfied in a unique and memorable way. This creates pressure on marketers to push themselves harder—not just to become category leaders, but to redefine their categories altogether.

Sometimes, over-delivery in a consumer experience can be a broad, meaningful, and often generous gesture that explodes categorization. There is a restaurant in Montréal called *Au Pied de Cochon* that would set alarm bells ringing at heart foundations around the world. It is an epicurean delight that takes considerations of what fatty content in food is safe and tosses them out the window. Instead, it celebrates rich, artery-clogging gourmet food in a way that thumbs its nose at convention. Its signature dish is *poutine au fois gras*, a mixture of French fries, gravy, cheese curds, and goose liver. The meal over-delivers by mixing a lowbrow fast food (**poutine** is a staple of Québécois cuisine—a lethally delicious combination of fries, gravy, and cheese curds) with a highbrow food (*foie gras,*) and standing the politically correct view of fine dining on its head. Of course, you don't eat it every day, and, clearly, it's not "heart smart." But walk into the warm, cheery *Au Pied de Cochon* on a cold, snowy Montréal night, and nothing melts your chilly insides like throwing caution to the wind by ordering it.

Volvo's success is a result of over-delivery on security. In reality, few drivers have required all the many, many safety features offered by Volvo. Wouldn't drivers be just as safe with only a few of them? And yet, Volvo's over-riding dedication is continuing proof of its outstanding commitment.

adidas Originals offers incredible variety and exclusivity, but do they really have to produce 2,400 shoe varieties? If you attempt to deliver on the promise of originality in a meaningful way, the answer is "yes."

Not every one of Apple's innovations is a financial success. However, without this over-delivery of new products and design, Apple would not mean what it does to its growing constituency.

We're fond of a U.K. fast food chain called Pret A Manger. Pret A Manger's goal is to topple the industrial food complex one convert at a time. So it jars consumers out of the fast-food mold by over-delivering on sustainable practices—from using unbleached cardboard sandwich wraps and biodegradable, corn-based plastic packaging for salads, to offering Rachel's Organic Milk in your latte.

One could argue that American Apparel's success is due to its over-delivery of a rebellious, anti-authoritarian attitude. The brand defies convention and challenges conventional ideas of beauty and propriety by using unglamorous civilians as models, striking soft-core poses in down-market bedrooms and basements. At the same time, it thumbs its nose at convention by loudly opposing sweatshop practices.

Although over-delivery can stand alone as a subset of EPO, it is often tied to other engines of Conversational Capital.

The creation of a powerful and memorable icon can result from over-delivery of design. We spoke about how Red Bull's can has become iconic. Later, we mentioned how Red Bull's founders spent a year working on that design. Clearly, some would have considered that investment of time during startup "a bit much," and yet, the product's success speaks for itself.

Rituals can sometimes be created by transforming banal behavior through over-delivery. Even a gesture as small as placing a lime into a bottle of beer can be considered over-delivery because that small gesture reinvents a category. Put a wedge of lime into a bottle of beer, and that beer becomes something like a cocktail. Initiation encourages us to over-deliver on one aspect of an experience or another, rendering it more challenging. For people used to drinking from a drip coffee maker, for instance, the perception of an espresso machine might be that it over-delivers on operational complexity.

Relevant Sensory Oddity hinges on the over-delivery of surprise and sensual stimulation. Jones Soda and method would not stand out if the people who make them decided to play it safe and deliver within preconceived expectations. Similarly, had Urban Outfitters under-delivered in terms of theming and presentation, it would be indistinguishable from any number of me-too retailers.

If this is confusing, we repeat that we are not discussing a rigorous system in this book. Conversational Capital is sinuous and liquid—often, its various engines inform one another, and categories can blend.

Whether it stands alone or blends with other engines, over-delivery is always tied to meaning. As we can see from the examples cited, it consistently tells us something about the consumer experience in question. Over-delivery does not mean over-reaching or over-stating. Simply going further or doing more won't create Conversational Capital if the gesture is essentially meaningless.

Most people use Microsoft Word. It wouldn't be surprising to learn that a large segment of these users find the program "over-stuffed." Are you familiar with that annoying little assistant that pops up and asks if you want help while you are writing—the one that folds up and waves at you before it mercifully disappears from the screen after you shut it off? What were these people thinking? Like an annoying salesperson who crowds you before you've asked for help, a function like this makes all kinds of mistaken assumptions about what you need or want as a writer.

In the end, over-delivery, like any engine of Conversational Capital, challenges us not to consider consumer behavior in a vacuum. Instead, its success lies in our ability to discern how we can turn meaning into a fulcrum for deeper connection.

WHO TOLD US TO WASTE OUR TIME WITH OBSERVATIONS, ANYWAY?

You know, we were doing fine before we put this book together. And yet, we have been compelled to over-deliver and try to stand out by creating Conversational Capital. You didn't expect it, and yet (we hope), it's filling a need. Even if it were a purely quixotic attempt (it's not), we'd stand out.

SUMMING UP

Over-delivery is an aspect of EPO. It's what happens when brands make an experience feel special by going much further than they have to in terms of customer satisfaction. Over-delivery occurs when consumer experiences include features that anticipate needs and desires consumers haven't even thought they would want but end up loving. In the end, it can be understood as an attitude: the desire to be the best and keep improving, just for the sake of it.

QUESTIONS FOR DISCUSSION

Can there ever be too much of a good thing?

Although it's good to transcend customer expectations and to constantly seek improvement, is it possible to be over-eager, and to push consumers too far? The answer seems to be "yes." We've all experienced the over-friendly waiter or the too-attentive salesperson. Sometimes, we just like to be left alone. The success of over-delivery depends on knowing how to listen and how to truly discern "white spaces" of opportunity. If you're really good, your customers probably expect you to surprise and delight them.

Where's the dividing line between genius and just being a nuisance? Your opinion will help us trace it.

Isn't customer satisfaction enough?

We don't believe it is, because a satisfied customer is not necessarily a vocal and supportive client. As we go into at greater length elsewhere in this book, customer satisfaction is a "green fee:" It's the least you have to do to stay in business. For Conversational Capital to happen, you have to get consumers deeply enthusiastic. And over-delivery is one way to get them there.

12.

MYTHS

Myths are foundation stories; the meta-narratives that shape and inform our culture. These stories encapsulate who we are, where we came from, and what we aspire to. Because traditional myths contain supernatural and fantastic elements, we sometimes think of them as "pretend stories," as in the term "urban myth." Although myths might contain fiction, they invariably reveal some important truth about us.

That's why, in our view, myth is one of the most important engines of Conversational Capital. If a consumer experience is permeated by myth, it is likely informed by a powerful, coherent story. Stories create resonance and salience and are the basic currency of identity formation. Myths are stories that tell us who we are.

Many Americans, for instance, perceive themselves as rugged, self-reliant, and free. These values are embedded in the United States' root narrative or founding myth: the American Revolution. Every other story about America begins with this central, shaping event. From it came the Declaration of Independence and Bill of Rights, touchstones of American philosophy and outlook. America's vision of itself as the "land of the free" was made possible by the revolution.

That myth is so strong that all other stories about America are measured against it. Any consideration of the U.S. weighs the country's real-life achievements or failings against that ideal. It is what gives America its distinct character and powerful identity.

The neighbor to the north of the U.S. provides an interesting contrast. Canada evolved as a country more slowly, in large part through negotiation and compromise. Without a revolution of its own, Canada doesn't have a founding myth. It might be a great place to live and might be respected internationally, but Canada has always had trouble defining itself.

Like nations and cultures, families have founding myths. Yours may be the old-money family that is forever either living up to its past expectations and achievements, or surpassing them. Or, you might be the product of an immigrant family, the inheritor of a founding myth that says "We have come here to make a better life for ourselves and to redefine who we are in the world," while trying to respect the weight of your inherited past.

Individuals have personal myths. We might see ourselves as radical progressives, conservatives, bohemians, nomads, artists, ordinary Joes, healers, victims, and so on. How we act and relate to others is informed by these founding personal myths, too.

It makes sense, then, that myth is such a critically important engine of Conversational Capital. Integrating myth into an experience gives it existential weight by grounding it in the identity-formation process.

We have observed that the source of myth can be both internal and external. By "internal," we mean stories that were integral to how the experience developed (endogenously). By external, we mean stories that are originally outside of and independent of the experience, and then get absorbed into it (exogenously).

Let's consider some examples of internal myths. Most Mac users are familiar with Apple's founding myth. This hallmark of independent thinking and reinvention was started by two young men with no money, but plenty of good ideas. When Mac users sit down in front of their computers, they do so in the context of that root narrative. Somewhere in the back of our minds, we hope that we are as creative, inventive, and free as Steve Jobs and Steve Wozniak.

adidas is rooted in the myth of the dedicated craftsman. It was founded by Adi Dassler, who began his career by hand-crafting shoes for all athletes, no matter how exotic the sport. His dedication to crafting shoes that enhanced athletic performance led him to personally design footwear for some of the highest-performing and most beloved athletes of the twentieth century. Not every adidas wearer is familiar with Dassler's story, of course, but adidas gains credibility because of the power of this underlying narrative.

Pret A Manger's founding in London is the stuff of myth. Here is how it tells the story of its founders: "Pret opened in London in 1986. College friends, Sinclair and Julian, made proper sandwiches using natural, preservative-free ingredients. The two of them had woefully little experience in the world of business. They created the sort of food they craved but couldn't find anywhere else. Because Pret is private, we don't face the same pressure to grow that a public company does. We will develop slowly, one shop at a time. There are about 150 Pret shops at the moment. Most of them are in the UK. We turn over roughly 150 million pounds a year and would like to make 9 percent profit but haven't yet. One day we will."

Innocent Drinks' founders tell their story—which is essentially about accountability—this way: "In fact, being accountable to our customers is something that is in our blood. In the summer of 1998, when we had developed our first smoothie recipes but were still nervous about giving up our proper jobs, we bought £500 worth of fruit, turned it into smoothies, and sold them from a stall at a little music festival in London. We put up a big sign saying 'Do you think we should give up our jobs to make these smoothies?' and put out a bin saying 'Yes' and a bin saying 'No' and asked people to put the empty bottle in the right bin. At the end of the weekend, the 'Yes' bin was full, so we went in the next day and resigned."

The Ben and Jerry's experience is rooted in the myth of the socially responsible vision and entrepreneurial free thinking of its namesake founders.

Internal myths can also be historical. Kellogg's cereals and Quaker Oats oatmeal provide good examples. Both food preparations were first developed as healthful solutions by Americans with a certain Puritanical bent. They were meant to be good for you. Each time you see the smiling, healthy-looking Quaker on the simple Quaker Oats packaging, you are potentially reminded of this founding narrative. The same is true for the relatively unchanging, clean lines of the Corn Flakes box. That myth of healthful, clean living still sticks to these iconic products, whatever their actual health benefits might be.

Sometimes, brands have no founding internal myths. Yet, through the mysterious operations of culture, they come to take on mythical associations. Myths become projected onto brands. The smart ones let it happen. The smartest run with it.

Think of the myth of the secret ingredient. Coke has long kept one of the ingredients of its soft drink formula a secret. There was a time—before Coke began implementing the strategy of incremental differentiation that has led to a seemingly endless stream of sub-brands—when that cloak of mystery had somehow made the brand seem more special. More recently, Red Bull has become another brand that makes use of the myth. One can of Red Bull is considered to be as energizing as four cups of coffee. What makes this possible is the presence of Taurine, an active ingredient whose nature is not as fully understood as caffeine. In both cases, a certain obscurity enables users to project their own theories and fancies into the equation. Trying to solve the mystery keeps consumers talking.

We like how American Express has made good use of a prevailing cultural myth with the introduction of the American Express Centurion Card (also known as the Black American Express Card). If you're a high net-worth individual and want to go skydiving at midnight tonight in Zambia, the concierge service at American Express' Elite Centurion Card might be able to arrange it for you. The card is available by invitation and is purported to require a minimum annual spending of $250,000. American Express Centurion customers have been rumored to have purchased Bentley automobiles with just a swipe of the card. Centurion holders have also made purchases well in excess of $1 million without a credit check. The card has no limit: Legend has it that the largest purchase ever made on it exceeded $30 million for a private jet.

In terms of Conversational Capital, what is most interesting about this card is that it existed in fiction before it ever did in reality. The black American Express card was an urban myth. People would talk about a special black card that gave .V.I.P.s unlimited spending power and all-hours access to high-end stores. The fact was that the card didn't exist. But the story had such tremendous aspirational power and cultural legs that American Express recognized a good thing when they saw it.

What would be the best way to incorporate the power of myth into your product or experience? The answer lies in the fact that myths are meant to tell us what your brand is fundamentally about.

Ask yourself what your brand is about. Is it about speed? Is it about comfort? Is it about health? Innovation? Peace of mind? Surprise? Escape? Social responsibility? Good times?

Then ask yourself: Is there a story hidden in your brand history that could speak to the hearts and minds of consumers? Can it be genuinely integrated into your brand experience or communications in any way?

Do you have a founding narrative? Is it still meaningful? It might be that your root narrative has been diluted or has become less relevant over the years. The Ford Motor Company is a great example. Henry Ford's introduction of the Model T—the world's first mass-produced motor vehicle—was a useful myth for decades. Because Ford was a mass-production pioneer, the firm could stake out a leadership position when mass production was the leading paradigm. With time, however, some of the drawbacks of mass production became evident in the design and fabrication of motor vehicles. The Ford name became an acronym for shoddy construction ("Found on the Road Dead," "Fix or Repair Daily," and so on). The founding myth, once an asset, became a liability. Word-of-mouth information about Ford went from positive to negative.

There is another aspect of Henry Ford's story that is, perhaps, less well known. Early in the history of his burgeoning enterprise, Ford clashed with fellow investors about the pricing of his cars. Henry Ford was resolute that his automobiles should be affordable to as many people as possible. Because he kept his vehicles inexpensive, more people could purchase them and enjoy the benefits of independent motor transportation. Because he insisted on it, car ownership was democratized to the benefit of more than just the upper classes.

Putting yourself on the line for the benefit of all is a good story. It's also a great founding myth. If Ford were to find a credible way to renew that promise, it could turn Conversational Capital back in its favor and breathe new life into the brand.

We end this section with a good-natured warning. Human beings love myth, and we tend to see it everywhere, even in places where it was never intended. So it's important to control any potential carriers of myth that your brand has, or they can control you. A good example of this is the half-moon symbol found on Procter & Gamble products. The symbol is innocent enough, though its origins are somewhat mysterious. Some years ago, conspiracy theorists began to interpret the symbol as a sign that Procter & Gamble was part of a satanic cult. The story soon spread, of course, and led to negative word-of-mouth that the company is still working hard to dispel. (At the time of this writing, Procter & Gamble is settling a suit centered on the *soi-disant* satanic symbol.)

Another famous example is the urban legend that Walt Disney was cryogenically frozen upon his death. The myth, completely false, probably arose from the fact that Disney was a private person and a technical innovator. His wish for privacy led to the details of his death and funeral being kept relatively quiet. His reputation for technical innovation let people fill in the blanks creatively. True or not, the creepy story of frozen Walt is probably on the minds—and lips—of many who visit Disney World every day.

BEFORE WE WROTE THIS BOOK, WE CUT A DEAL WITH SATAN

Man, that's so untrue. But if you've ever listened to blues music, you probably know the story about Robert Johnson, who was rumored to have sold his soul to a dark stranger at the Crossroads in exchange for his revolutionary guitar skills. True or not, the Crossroads story is a founding myth of rock 'n roll, which, for decades before it became your parents' music, was all about danger and transgression. The myth is still powerful enough to drive accountants, lawyers, and even some advertising people to "get crazy" at megaband reunion tours.

We did make a deal with our publisher, who has a goatee but no horns, tail, or pitchfork that we know of.

SUMMING UP

Myth might be the most critical engine of Conversational Capital because it embodies a brand story. Essentially, stories set brands apart because they are so important in the identity-forming and affirmation process. We are the sum of our stories and we look to myth to provide them. If your brand is powered by myth, it might be all you need.

QUESTIONS FOR DISCUSSION

Can myth be manufactured?

Most myths are naturally occurring. In brand stories, they come from the lives of founders or from brand history. Because they are powerful stories to begin with, they have probably asserted themselves organically.

However, there are cases when myths can be invented from whole cloth. Häagen-Dazs is resonant with echoes of Scandaniavian richness and good taste—but it's owned by Pillsbury and made in New Jersey. Sleeman beer was represented by an owner of the same name and told a story of tradition and continuity. However, the fact is that John Sleeman is only a distant relative of the creator of a beverage that was out of production for decades before he revived it.

Examples abound and beg a further question: Are manufactured myths as powerful as naturally occurring myths? We suggest that it's all a matter of how that myth resonates—or is made to resonate—within the whole consumer experience.

13.

RELEVANT SENSORY ODDITY (RSO)

We have shut down our senses. Because so much of our urban and suburban infrastructure has been designed for optimum functionality in the automobile age, let's face it—it's not very nice to look at, especially in North America. Sitting in our cars and rolling past strip malls, highway exit signs, and off-ramps, we've learned to tune out much of our environment. The fact that a great many individuals spend much of their working lives in spaces where function has erased the beauty of form has contributed to an overall numbing of the senses.

In our quest for cleanliness and order, we have reduced the variety of odors in our environments. By piping in music to the point of over-saturation, we have also encouraged a general lack of attention to our aural environments. On the tactile level, we favor smooth, even surfaces that do not draw too much attention to themselves in a "look but don't touch" world.

No wonder, then, that relevant sensory oddity can have so much power in creating Conversational Capital. RSO challenges our tendency to shut out our environment. In a world of ambient homogeneity, RSO startles our senses back to life.

As we enter an era of greater customization, we might, gratefully, be moving beyond the sensory neutrality that was so much a piece of mass industrialization. In supermarkets and in stores, the shelves are packed with increasing varieties of products that appeal to all our senses. Those products that most stand out in their very form and shape are those that command our greatest attention.

That's why we consider RSO to be, along with myth, a crucial marker of Conversational Capital. Product design and marketing has for too long been dominated by visual appeal. Although this is certainly important, it has underleveraged the fact that human beings have five senses. We see, hear, touch, taste and smell—and if a consumer experience can appeal to our complete faculties, it becomes all the more impactful and potentially meaningful.

When our senses are challenged, we never forget. Simply put, we are removed from our desensitized perceptions of reality and transported to a more extraordinary place.

No wonder, then, that some of the most-talked about brands routinely jar our senses. Bear in mind, however, that we have called this engine of Conversational Capital *relevant* sensory oddity. Just jarring the senses isn't enough. RSO happens when the senses are stimulated and challenged in a manner that's intelligent and salient to the consumer experience. We could have printed this book on green paper. It would certainly have drawn attention, but would it necessarily have been resonant? In RSO, as with Conversational Capital writ large, meaning rules over bombast.

Examples can extend from the sublime to the very routine, and everywhere in between:

- NOKIA has distinguished itself from other cell phone manufacturers through the sound of its trademark ring. For some, this rolling, descending chime is so unique and arresting that they refuse to switch because of it.

- When Tony Chi designed the rooms at Skylofts at MGM Grand, his intention was to create spaces that *felt* as well as looked high-end. You can run your hand along the walls and furnishings and feel a range of textures and temperatures. This, combined with clean lines, helps to create a Zen-like feeling of "relaxed alertness" high above the hustle and bustle of the Strip.

- The Volkswagen Beetle became an automobile icon because it looked so different from anything that came before it. Today, the smart and, to a certain extent, the MINI Cooper, flaunt qualities opposite to the tendencies of "how cars should look" and draw similar attention.

- Philippe Starck takes everyday objects like corkscrews and accentuates their oddities. At Starck-designed hotels, one's sense of scale is constantly challenged through the addition of such elements as gigantically oversized flowerpots and avant-garde chandeliers.

- The Brian Eno-designed sound that greets the opening of every Windows operating system is meant to draw our attention. By appealing to our sense of hearing in a unique way, it is trying to tell us that we are about to enter a more exalted, voluptuous sphere of activity.

- The beautiful blue color and distinct shape of the Bombay Sapphire gin bottle may have as much to do with the popularity of the brand among trend-setters as it does with its taste. Similarly, Absolut vodka has intelligently leveraged the distinct shape of its bottle to market itself for decades.

- Rolex watches are much-prized. Could it be in large part because they are simply bigger and heavier than other watches and, therefore, *feel* more substantial?

- Alamo Drafthouse has radically reconfigured the cinema experience. This Texas repertory theater housed in a renovated period building serves up serious cinema and food. Filmgoers can sit at tables and order from waiters during screenings. The meals offered are often keyed to the film being screened (*Like Water for Chocolate* = gourmet Mexican food). Local bands accompany silent movies.

- Central Market is a Texas-based specialty grocer whose stores typically occupy more than 75,000 sq. ft. They do away with the aisles normally found in grocery stores and instead organize product offerings in the form of a sensory and zonal journey akin to a trip through IKEA.

- The Amanyara is part of the Aman resort chain, which draws people with a shared lifestyle from the world over. That lifestyle is about a lust for faraway cultures and an appetite for pampering and a deep appreciation of elegance and creativity. This resort in the Turks and Caicos Islands suspends time and space by deliberately avoiding Caribbean references in its décor and service offering. Instead, design leans to Asian influences, and a significant portion of the staff are Oriental. So while you are actually four hours away by plane from New York City, you completely lose your sense of time and place, thus increasing your ability to relax.

- Jones Soda comes in glass bottles, with black and white packaging, is flavored with cane sugar, and comes in a staggering array of surprising flavors—at every step redefining what we should expect from widely available commercial beverages.

- Urban Outfitters deliberately jams the impulse to order and propriety that unite most clothing retailers. Its storefront is composed of smashed glass; its displays and merchandise are grungy, anti-authoritative, and often controversial.

- Abercrombie & Fitch is an RSO champion. It creates an anti-retail store environment intended to appeal to its age 15 to 30 preppy grunge market—and keep everyone else out. Shoppers can't see inside the store while outside it. Inside the store is very dimly lit, and music is kept aggressively loud. Portraits of half-dressed models grace the walls. Even a distinctive aroma fills the air.

- With retail outlets that hearken back to the glory days of the department store, Nordstrom challenges both our senses and our jaded conceptions. The pianist in the atrium, the dining experience in its cafes, the wide, bright aisles that encourage exploration; the lack of pretentiousness and intimidation fostered by an open, accessible culture of service; these traits make shopping surprisingly surprising.

- Herman Miller's Aeron Chair has become a $950 fixture in many executive suites, due in no small part to the fact that it defies pre-existing notions of design. It is at once a symbol of avant-garde industrial design and ergonomic comfort. It includes a component that is made in three different sizes, depending on the size of your derriere. It is a see-through chair without upholstery that costs close to a thousand dollars.

- IDEO, a California-based design consultancy, has become an international success in large part by leveraging the power of RSO. Its long list of innovations includes the first Apple mouse, the Palm V, Bank of America's "Keep the Change" service, the world's first notebook computer, and the Swiffer—each one of them experiences in joyful sensual discontinuity from the pre-existing category norm.

- In a world where ice cream vendors constantly seek to lead through choice and variety, Pinkberry is a California-based retailer of tart, non-fat frozen yogurt that has generated enviable word-of-mouth success by taking the opposite tack, and offering only three flavors: original, green tea, and coffee.

- Innocent Drinks makes healthy juices and drives home its uniqueness by packaging its product in six ounce bottles. The message is clear and relevant: In an era where servings are enormous, Innocent is about moderation.

- Guests at Four Seasons hotels are greeted by remarkable floral displays in the lobby. These displays go farther than any other hotel in their sensual evocation of opulence and elegance.

- Kettle Chips are notoriously harder to open than any other brand. This sensory discontinuity is not without purpose: If you didn't have a hard time opening the bag, you might doubt Kettle's promise of extra freshness.

- Heinz ketchup seems to slow time itself down. To not have the ketchup pour out of its container at an excruciatingly halting pace, insiders have learned that you have to knock the bottle at the neck (thereby creating tribalism and initiation to go with your RSO and French fries). And yet, this potential brake on consumer satisfaction has helped to make Heinz an iconic brand.

RSO as a factor in consumer experience often extends, not just to the experience itself, but to how that experience is promoted—which is fine by us, as we firmly believe the two should be part of an integrated and continuous whole.

Marketing communications would simply not exist without an element of RSO. Every effort from direct marketing envelopes to billboards has been designed, in some fashion, to stand out and capture our attention. The most successful do it with wit, flair, and relevance.

We note that changes in 3-D media and interactive media are providing new opportunities to create RSO without necessitating an investment in dramatic structural overhauls. Over-sized interactive screens and installations and innovative projections are already helping to creative surprising, immersive experiences, and the future looks even more promising.

As always, our observations about the engines of Conversational Capital come with some provisos. In the case of relevant sensory oddity, they are the following:

- The alteration of sensory touchpoints should be related to the product in question. The Beetle was a revolution not only of form, but also of function. Significantly, much of its revolutionary shape came out of the fact that its engine was in the back of the car. If the process of having our senses challenged does ultimately have a connection to the experience itself—if it feels like an add-on—the result might feel fake and bombastic, rather than organic and surprising.

- Design and sensory innovation must be backed by product efficacy. Bombay Sapphire gin might come in a bottle that looks and feels cool, but it has to taste at least as good as a competing brand. If Abercrombie & Fitch was all sensual overload, but the clothes were out of step with fashion and poorly made, it would be a champion of bombast, not RSO.

- Relevant sensory oddity will get you talked about by reminding consumers that they are experiencing something out-of-the-ordinary. To have real and long-lasting effect, however, that extra-ordinariness has to extend beyond what you promise about an experience. *It has to be ingrained in the experience itself.*

WOULDN'T IT BE COOL IF THIS BOOK TURNED TO LIQUID IN YOUR HANDS?

And the print just stayed on your skin? The experience would be so out of the ordinary, you'd never forget it. That's what RSO is all about: enriching your experience, with relevant, surprising twists. If we could have managed the book-turning-to-liquid trick, we would have done it to drive our point home.

SUMMING UP

RSO stands for relevant sensory oddity. It can be observed when a consumer experience surprises and delights a full range of senses. It recognizes that human beings see, touch, hear, taste, and feel and communicates with them on that level. However, doing so in a manner that is relevant, and resonates with the consumer experience in a meaningful way, is key.

QUESTIONS FOR DISCUSSION

Isn't RSO messy?

Clearly, when you start to speak about manipulating the way things smell, taste, and feel in an environment, it could make some people nervous. Mass market North American culture has become deflavorized for so long that this reaction is understandable. However, neutral homogeneity doesn't reflect the full range of experience. We are sensual creatures, and leading brands have recognized this by daring to up the sensual ante. True, some people find any kind of change or challenges to the senses "weird," but are product manufacturers and marketers making a mistake by appealing to what might be a tremulous few, in hopes of not offending? What do you think?

14.

ICONS

The word icon has its origins in art history. Strictly speaking, an icon is the product of the Eastern Orthodox Christian Church—a depiction, in oils, on a wooden surface, and of a religious subject (often of the Virgin Mary and Infant Jesus). Actually the Greek word for morals, icon has since taken on a much wider meaning in current English usage. We now take it to mean something like a symbol, but larger and more powerful in meaning and significance.

To us, an icon is still tied to its origins in religious art: It's a symbol or sign of something deeper, larger, and more complex. It has the power to distill a larger web of meaningful connections and associations into a single expression.

Icons are more complex than mere signs. Signs have clear, undisputed meanings. When you see a stop sign, you just stop: You don't spend time philosophizing about its meaning. Icons, by contrast, have rich sets of associations that encourage us to think about what they mean. So, where signs are triggers for action, icons encourage thought and reflection.

Words are extremely useful. (Without them, you'd be holding a sheaf of bound, blank, white pages in your hand, undoubtedly drawing a few curious glances.) However, they require some time and effort to decode. Icons are extremely efficient *heuristics*—carriers of information that enable us to decode a lot of information quickly.

We can turn almost any part of our experience into something iconic under the right circumstances. Consider how the following can and have become icons.

PEOPLE

A person becomes an icon when they symbolize something larger than themselves. This is the result of actions, associations, or events that drive an individual into the spotlight. When we think of iconic people, we think of all they stand for. Some examples follow:

John Wayne—The cowboy icon. A symbol of the rugged, outdoorsy, self-reliant, independent, American male.

Marilyn Monroe—An icon of glamour and erotic energy, with an undercurrent of tragic sexuality.

Gandhi—A spiritual leader, pacifist, and innovator.

Bruce Lee—Intelligent, disciplined, and a man of action.

Jimi Hendrix—An icon of the psychedelic swinging 60s, androgyny, racial danger, invention, explosive creativity, and virtuosity.

Pelé—Athletic excellence, a symbol of Brazil's limitless potential, and the uniting, international appeal of soccer.

Bill Gates—An icon of the nerd as conquering hero.

BUILDINGS

In some cases, buildings can become more than just structures. Through architectural considerations and the force of history, they become symbols, too.

Think of the Eiffel Tower in Paris. For many, it is a symbol of all things French. For others, it is a symbol of "belle époque"— Europe in all its hope and invention.

The Empire State Building or Chrysler Building in New York City have similar iconic power. We think of them as symbolizing all the energy, hustle, daring, and promise of the American experience. (The World Trade Center, sadly, became the opposite, indicating the power of icons to take on both brightly positive and terribly negative associations.)

The iconic power of buildings is well understood today. Think of how Bilbao has redefined itself as a cultural destination by commissioning a museum by Frank Gehry or how the bustling city of Dubai benefited from the post-modern aesthetic of the Burj al Arab, a terrifically iconic seven-star hotel.

Whereas certain buildings can become iconic, some cities have become icons, too. New York and Paris are cases in point (American hustle, European sophistication), as are Las Vegas (sin city), Hong Kong (the rise of the Asian tiger), and Rio de Janeiro (sun-drenched libertinism).

PHYSICAL GEOGRAPHY

As with cities, certain aspects of landscape can become iconic. The Rocky Mountains are icons of open air, freedom, and majesty. Rivers are icons of freedom and movement. The sandy Caribbean Beach is ripe with symbolic associations that add up to much more than sand and salt water—something high-end real estate developers clearly recognize.

OBJECTS

Sigmund Freud, interpreting a patient's dream, once famously remarked, "Madam, sometimes a cigar is just a cigar." At other times, it is much more. Beyond phallic symbolism, the cigar has become an icon of conservative, unapologetic masculinity, and power. Other everyday objects, from wine glasses to cowboy boots to leather jackets, have also become iconically charged. No longer mere things, they become symbols we wear, hold, and variously use.

ICONIC PRODUCT DESIGN

We firmly believe that icons can be created by unique, powerful design—something that, unfortunately, too many companies are reluctant to pay for. By under-investing in graphic, architectural, industrial, and ultimately, experiential design, companies run the risk of depriving themselves of an important engine, indeed engines, of Conversational Capital.

The Red Bull can has become a modern-day icon. We note that it took Dietrich Mateschitz and Johannes Kastner more than a year during the company's start-up phase to design the can—after much discussion about what angle the transversal line across it should run at. (They eventually settled on 45 degrees.) Some might have argued that this micro-management of packaging minutiae was an over-investment in time and resources, but the result clearly speaks for itself.

Through such care and attention, product and package design can take on iconic power. When they do, consumption experiences can become associated with themes as sweeping and meaningful as national character, cultural values, and historical trends. Look at a photo of the Volkswagen Beetle, and you associate it with the cultural revolution of the 1960s and '70s. It was small when cars were big, curved where cars were boxy. Its engine was in the back; its trunk in the front. A more perfect vehicle for revolutionary aspiration was never made.

Similarly, the DeLorean was the perfect symbol for the materialistic excesses of the 1980s. The fact that its doors opened upward made it "iconically receptive," and a mark of status for the upwardly mobile. Today, cars like the MINI Cooper and Prius zig where other cars zag, opening themselves up for iconic empowerment by a culture concerned with style, perception, and environmental impact.

Iconic product design isn't limited to cars, of course.

We like to think that, in its form, *The New York Times* has become an icon. They must feel the same way at the *Times*, because they have cleaved to its iconic broadsheet, eight-column format, which, at a glance, encapsulates credibility, authority, and tradition.

What makes the Harley Davidson motorcycle different from, say, the more run-of-the-mill Honda or Yamaha? Over time, Harley has become the ultimate icon for the American psyche, emblematic of patriotism, masculinity, and fierce individualism, and nostalgia for the glory days.

The loft-like, multistory space at Urban Outfitters has become an icon of an intentionally trashy, hipster attitude. And Ben & Jerry's distinctive unbleached pint packaging and avant-garde flavor names speak volumes about the Vermont ice cream maker's hippie-inspired, alternative take on ice cream.

POWERED BY ASSOCIATION

Note that all the product icons cited have strong associations. In the case of Cirque du Soleil's Big Top, it is escape and renewal. With the Volkswagen Beetle, it was freedom and innovation. With Ben and Jerry's, it is unconventional thinking and social responsibility.

Not all icons retain the same degree of pull. Some evoke more resonant associations than others. Conversational Capital works best when you incorporate highly salient icons into your experience. As individuals, we like to stand for something. The experiences we engage in embody the values and ideas we aspire to represent. That's why we talk about them.

The most successful examples of icon incorporation are when the product not only includes iconic elements, but also is iconic *in and of itself.* This is what happened with the Volkswagen Beetle. It can even happen with the most humble household items.

Consider the recent introduction of the Swiffer. Intelligently conceived by IDEO in partnership with P&G, it makes dusting so easy and convenient that it actually becomes enjoyable and fulfilling. It has emerged as an icon of convenience, innovation, and practicality. It is a tissue paper-sized cloth in workaday packaging. Yet it is a great example of product as icon.

Not every product, however, is innovative and first in class. In advertising pioneer David Ogilvy's famous dichotomy, products fall into one of two classes. They are either original, or they are not. The Swiffer is original. The Private Label Swiffer knock-off at your corner grocery store is not. In Ogilvy's still widely respected theory, then, the marketer is left with two choices. If your product is original, simply speak to its originality. If your product is not, then you must communicate about it in an original way.

Clearly, if your product or experience is original and innovative, it probably lends itself more easily to iconic expression. Find what it is that sets your product apart and use that as a springboard, whether you are selling a new car or opening a new petting zoo. If, on the other hand, your product is a "me too" product, try to find something iconic to say or associate with it. If you are the first person in your product category to ask, "What does my product stand for? Why should consumers identify with it in a meaningful way? What icon best helps me communicate the answer to these questions?" You might, in the world of word-of-mouth communication, be perceived as category leader (even as a late entrant).

Think of what happened with Target stores in the U.S. Target occupied a position on the retail spectrum sandwiched between Wal-Mart and K-Mart. To stand out, Target chose to embrace design in discount retail by bringing in respected designers and labels. As a result, Target has become first in class in "cheap chic"—a position illustrated by the chain's hip and colorful iconography, and reflected in media coverage.

WHAT THE ICON PROMISES, YOU MUST DELIVER!

Conversational Capital isn't just about salient experiences. It's also about continuity and integrity of experience. What does that mean, exactly? It means that, if you make a promise about something, that promise has to hold up throughout the entire experience. If you say one thing and deliver another, the experience becomes hollow and disappointing—and subject to negative word-of-mouth.

So choose your icons carefully! Your icon must be truly representative of the experience as a whole. If it's appliquéd and false, consumers will recognize it for the window-dressing it is.

And nobody has anything good to say about a fake.

SUMMING UP

Icons are signs and symbols that are rich in evocative power and associations. Almost anything can take on the shorthand power of an icon: places, buildings, people, logos, labels, and more. The key is that these icons have to evoke a compelling brand story.

QUESTIONS FOR DISCUSSION

Is a yield sign an icon?

A yield sign evokes a story of a kind, doesn't it? It clearly and effectively communicates a message. But it can't actually be considered an icon because it doesn't evoke more than simple directions. You can distinguish signs from icons by depth of evocation. Are there any cases in the examples we've cited where we might have tested this distinction?

15.

TRIBALISM

What tribe do you belong to? Which group of people do you feel most at home with? With whom do you truly identify?

These are important questions, because group affiliation is a massive part of identity determination. And, as we pointed out previously, identity formation is a central component of the narrative exercise we call Conversational Capital.

Some tribes, such as our families, choose us. This is the static form of tribalism. At the same time, there are tribal affiliations we buy into when we exercise our individual tastes, preferences, and principles. As marketers, we're interested in this more dynamic form of tribalism because it takes place in the realm of consumer choice.

Conversational Capital grows when you facilitate the formation of tribes and tribal behavior. Certainly, knowing that an experience has been designed to please a certain group makes that service or product more communicable within that group. In other words, if you know that people out there like what you like, you are almost definitely going to be inclined to spread the word when you're enthusiastic about it. Just as a real-life virus can spread most rapidly among people who share the same space, consumer talk can spread fastest among people who share the same headspace.

Anyone who's read Malcolm Gladwell's *The Tipping Point* is familiar with the importance of what he calls "innovators" and "connectors." These are the individuals in groups who help establish (innovators) and spread (connectors) certain forms of behavior in social groups. Tribalism leverages the power of connectors to spread the word about your experience widely and rapidly.

To see how this can work, consider the Internet. The Web has made it easier than ever for members of various consumer tribes to connect. Significantly, some web-based businesses have worked tribalist assumptions into the business model itself. Amazon.com is a clear example of this. Each time you return to the online store and make a purchase (or even simply explore), you are told: "Users who enjoyed this title also enjoyed X." These lists of suggested titles are generated by algorithms, predicated on the idea that your tastes must be shared and that you must belong to a tribe. If someone in your tribe liked Product A, and you liked Product A, chances are good you'll like Product B, if your fellow tribesperson liked Product B, too. What holds true for businesses like Amazon holds true for other web-based businesses such as eBay, iTunes, and Netflix.

But how can you maximize the power of tribalism outside of the entertainment business or the Internet? One thing that is clear from our observations is that the power of tribal affiliation is strongest when it occurs spontaneously. Tribes naturally form around shared feelings, interests, and needs. The best brands piggyback on these when they already exist.

Consider the branding success stories that have leveraged the power of tribalism.

- The success of the Alamo Drafthouse cinema chain would not have occurred had a tribe not been present to establish and sustain its growth. The Drafthouse explicitly appeals to film buffs who want to gather in a place where they can share their interests and points of view with people (something they could never experience the same way on, say, an Internet fan forum).

- The sense of tribalism among Harley Davidson riders is strong enough to enable regular gatherings of huge throngs of riders at Harley Conventions across the U.S.

- Build-a-Bear is a retail workshop concept that invites people to participate in the creation of custom-made teddy bears together. Simply showing up at the store puts you in contact with others who share your interests and fosters community and exchange.

- The aforementioned Central Market appeals directly to "foodies," fine food aficionados who recognize one another for their common sensibilities and who, in many cases, want to share their enthusiasms.

- Guitar Center leverages the natural sense of tribalism that exists among musicians. It has created a chain of stores that is staffed by people who are as passionate about music as their customers are.

- Urban Outfitters has become a center for tribal interaction by creating a retail space that combines the necessary elements for hipster life (apparel, shoes, furniture, music, and books), with an unusual selection of luxury brands (Lacoste, Evisu, Diesel, True Religion, and Seven for All Mankind). Customers gather to browse through a self-expressive line of identity-shaping products that foster tribalism in a number of adolescent subcultures (namely gothic, preppy, skater, retro, and bohemian).

Note that in all the examples cited, tribes have formed organically where an experience that appeals to their shared interests has been created. They have been drawn to it by choice: No one has tried to force them together. Tribalism should be *allowed* to happen—it can't be manufactured.

There is an important distinction to be made here: Simply forming an affinity program is not fostering a sense of tribalism. Affinity programs are based on creating a relationship between a brand and individual users. Tribes form when people relate to one another, and consumer tribes form when a brand becomes part of that interaction. It's not the brand talking to you or me in separate conversations. It's you and me involved in a discussion with the brand—the three of us together, with equal footing in the group dynamic.

Affinity programs that force people into groups they have not expressed an interest in belonging to can be alienating, and this can drive people away from your brand. Clumsy direct marketers make this kind of mistake more often then they would like. For example, a major Canadian telephone company pushing discount long-distance rates made the faulty assumption that if someone on its list had a foreign-sounding name, the person in question was a recent immigrant. They sent a targeted mailing addressing that person as an immigrant who might want call his relatives in the home country at amazing low rates—blithely ignoring the reality that the recipient of said mailing had lived in Canada for almost 50 years and had little or nothing to do with the "home country." The end result is that the targeted recipient felt deeply insulted and came away with the (deserved) perception that the sender was out-of-touch with the nuanced cultural fabric of its market.

Simply put, it is better to find ways to let your target market express a sense of tribalism before you assume it exists.

The failure of the Canadian company cited might simply be that it operates according to the faulty assumptions of the top-down, mass-market paradigm. In a consumer environment that is increasingly niche-driven, peer-mediated, and horizontally organized, the line between producer and consumer is being erased. More and more, the producer and the consumer are organically connected by shared needs, interests, and feelings.

It happens with increasing frequency in the digital age, but this confluence of producer and user has always existed in some form. Readers of a certain age will remember commercials for the Hair Club for Men. The company, which sold a patented hair-weaving technology, positioned itself as the ideal solution for men who felt the perceived sting of male pattern baldness. A credible-looking spokesperson introduced a series of before-and-after pictures showing first follicly challenged men, and then, the lustrous, weaved do's they sported as members of the club.

What set the Hair Club for Men aside was the idea that rather than just feeling like random victims of a cruel fate, bald men could see themselves as a select group who understood one another's pain. The promise of mutual empathy gained tremendous credibility when, at the end of the commercial, the spokesperson held up a before-and-after picture of himself and revealed that, he, too, was a member of the club. The Hair Club took that credibility a step further in later commercials that revealed that the company's president was a member, as well. The Hair Club for Men's commercials became the fodder for a lot of humor at the time. Nevertheless, the company became part of the cultural fabric, talked about by many, and almost always with good humor (albeit ironic fondness in some cases). Certainly, for those men inclined to feel the Hair Club's pain, the company and its campaign were an unqualified success.

But there's a caution to be heeded here. Take tribalism too far, and you make it self-defeating. From music to film, to publishing, to any number of lifestyle products, the consumer environment is now filled with marketers that are creating products for like-minded consumers—for their tribes. These niches are becoming concentric, as consumers find their needs fulfilled more and more deeply by producers sensitive to their particular needs.

The dangers of this symbiotic relationship are two-fold:

- The long-term viability of a tribe can be challenged by changing tastes, the evolution of fashion, and the simple march of time. What niche consumers feel they absolutely need today, they might rapidly grow out of tomorrow. Marketers who pander slavishly to their tribe might find that the tribe has moved on and no longer needs them—and sooner than anyone expected.

- By increasingly narrowing the focus to cater to tribes, we might help tribes become too small to be sustainable.

TODAY'S TRIBE OF CHOICE CAN BECOME
TOMORROW'S SHRINERS CLUB

This is the peril of being too trendy. How can you avoid it? Here's another example involving Apple. If Apple had been content to rest on its success with the iPod, it could simply have redefined itself as the premiere manufacturer of personal music devices for the style-conscious. But its leaders knew that there were significant synergies to be leveraged in creating a wider tribe. That assumption drove the transformation of Apple from a "computer company" to a "lifestyle electronics solutions provider." Successful tribal marketers remain viable through changing styles and trends by keeping an ear to the ground. Rather than simply pander to the demands of the niche, they try to see where the next needs will be by being sensitive to what the market is saying. In the best cases, they hear the call of their own best instincts, too.

In other words, in the age of talk, they listen.

THERE ARE A LOT OF PEOPLE READING OVER YOUR SHOULDER RIGHT NOW

Symbolically, at least. We're writing this book for you, the individual reader. But we're also conscious that a lot of people out there share your concerns and preoccupations. There's not much a book can do to bring you closer together. That's why we created the Conversational Capital blog. By reading, contributing, and commenting on the blog, people like you can share your thoughts and opinions, and you can help us focus our thinking. As a member of the tribe, you participate in the evolution of the approach.

Just don't ask for a share of the royalties.

SUMMING UP

In essence, Conversational Capital occurs when brand stories become part of the identity formation and affirmation process. Determining which tribe you belong to is a bedrock component of that process. Tribalism takes place when consumer experiences draw the like-minded together in a quest for mutual discovery.

QUESTIONS FOR DISCUSSION

This is the 21st century. Am I really part of a tribe?

The word "tribe" can sound archaic. After all, we modern people are part of families, communities, business associations, political parties, and more. What the 21st century has revealed, however, is that even these social definitions can be porous and continually shifting. Tribalism actually speaks to what is individual in our tastes and desires and to how the consumer culture creates surprising associations. People from social groups that are against one another might be part of the same consumer tribe. Tribalism may, in fact, penetrate beyond arbitrary social categories to what fundamentally unites us.

Does that make consumer behavior seem more than it is? What have you observed about tribalism?

16.

ENDORSEMENT

When a trusted friend or someone you look up to endorses an experience, nothing is more likely to persuade you to try it. This is a chapter on the most powerful form of affirmation there is—peer-mediated endorsement.

Endorsement works when credible members of a tribe put their reputations on the line to stand behind an experience. Peer endorsement is as different from celebrity product endorsement as buzz is from Conversational Capital. Because top-down celebrity endorsement is bought and paid for, it can feel meaningless and hollow. In the rare instance, it *can* work, if the celebrity endorser is the right person, someone who embodies the brand (the case of Nike comes to mind). However, it can be an expensive proposition. And, often, this type of endorsement is fundamentally disconnected from the experience that is endorsed. It feels phony. Peer endorsement, on the other hand, is a natural and organic outcome of meaningful engagement with an experience. It has its roots in the deep satisfaction and relevance that turns consumers into brand advocates.

Remember what happened with the Planet Hollywood chain of restaurants? It provides an excellent cautionary tale about the wrong kind of endorsement. Owned in part by high-profile celebrities, it opened with great fanfare and success. Endorsements by these part owners, who routinely showed up at glitzy, red-carpet restaurant openings, drew a lot of attention and interest. Their presence created buzz. Unfortunately, it soon became apparent to Planet Hollywood visitors that the chain's celebrity ownership was mostly cosmetic. In reality, the experience of the product did not reflect the aura and appeal of its celebrity spokespersons. The result? As it tends to, buzz faded, and word-of-mouth about Planet Hollywood turned negative.

Compare this sad state of affairs to what happens when the people we call "local celebrities" (authorities in peer groups) endorse an experience. Local celebrities are similar to those Malcolm Gladwell calls influencers in *The Tipping Point*. These individuals—who can range from the guy in the ski shop who recommends a certain snowboard, to a well-liked sommelier, to a respected blogger—are taste makers. They are the authorities people in peer communities look to for cues.

This is what happened with Cirque du Soleil. Tastemakers—many of whom, ironically, were "genuine" celebrities—became early adopters and brand ambassadors.

Endorsement and tribalism are linked. When engineering Conversational Capital, you have to engage the critical mass of people you feel will:

- Find your experience meaningful.

- Have the authority to influence people in their peer group.

- Be naturally inclined to share their enthusiasm about your experience.

THIS BOOK BEGAN WITH CONVERSATIONS. WE HOPE IT STARTS MORE

It means a lot to us that you like this book. It will mean even more if you talk about it because your endorsement as peers is the most powerful support we can get. Peer endorsement—by word-of-mouth or through peer-mediated vehicles such as magazines and websites—carries more weight than anything you could pay for.

This is targeting at the micro level. Rather than imagine faceless demographic groups, you should aim to reach individuals at the DNA level. When you connect with them, endorsement should happen organically.

Endorsement, of course, can't make brand experiences meaningful or interesting. That is a product of the brand experience itself. But knowing that the right people have enjoyed an experience can give it an aura and promise that marketers must be on their guard to live up to.

SUMMING UP

Endorsement is not a matter of well-known people speaking for your consumer experience. Rather, it is a matter of consumers advocating on your behalf in a free and unsolicited manner. This is the most powerful form of marketing there is. However, endorsement comes with a built-in caveat. If you are endorsed, you need to live up to consumer support. If they recommend you to someone who is disappointed, they look bad, too.

QUESTIONS FOR DISCUSSION

Is endorsement just advocacy under another name?

No. As we indicated earlier, advocacy is a wonderful thing. However, Conversational Capital aims at more than advocacy. Advocates are great ambassadors. Endorsers are that and more. They are converts. They have made your experience part of their lifestyle. So the warning applies even more stringently to them. Treat them right, at your peril.

Does that sound like giving the consumer too much power?

17.

CONTINUITY

Positive word-of-mouth is the result of continuity between promise, image, and experience. Conventional marketing has always been preoccupied with the former. It tries to summarize what and how we are to think about an experience and communicate it in the most efficient way possible. As a result, the entire traditional advertising industry's work is focused on finding catchphrases and slogans such as the following:

- Refreshes the parts other beers cannot reach

- We try harder

- You can't top the copper-top

- We bring good things to life

- A diamond is forever

Coming up with a great tagline, however, isn't enough to get people to talk about you. Rather, word-of-mouth is a by-product of a dynamic relationship between your experience (who you are), how you communicate that experience (who you say you are), and how consumers feel about that experience (who people say you are).

If the opposite is true—if the three are disconnected—it can have a damaging effect because it compromises your credibility and more dangerously, the credibility of your customers.

Think about how it works. Having enjoyed an experience, a consumer tells other people about how good it was. Significantly, they stake their personal reputation on it. If the people they speak to enjoy it as well, the positive reputation of both referrer and referree increases.

As we stated previously, not all the engines of Conversational Capital have to be present. However, the positive feedback loop we call continuity *is the one engine of Conversational Capital whose presence is absolutely necessary*. Without continuity, Conversational Capital simply won't happen. A consumer contributes to a brand's reputation only insofar as he is confident that, in doing so, he won't look like a fool. Quite the contrary, in fact—they hope to appear more intelligent, interesting, sensitive, possessing of good taste, and so on in the reflected glow of the brand experience.

It's not much of a shift in thinking, but it's one not enough marketers have made yet: *Reputation isn't just about you.* Most marketers still stop at the idea that reputation is about their products. They don't consider how reputation and product use reflect on consumers.

Whether you create household goods or international entertainment blockbusters, reputation always has symbiotic power. It can't be over-stated: Smart product manufacturers and marketers are sensitive to how much a reputation, built through years of effort to deliver a consistently superior experience, reflects on those consumers.

What is your role in the equation, then? The way people talk about you has to be an organic by-product of a true connection between what you say your experience is and what your experience truly delivers. Think of how it works in life. You can't artificially turn your image into a talking point. If you say something like, "I'm known for how smart I am," or "People say I'm very funny," you are neither. To get people to say you are smart or funny, you have to *be* smart or funny in the first place. You can't just say you are.

It follows, then, that you can build continuity into your Conversational Capital by keeping an eye on the ultimate benefits of your product or experience. If you hope to get a standing ovation every time you perform, what can you do before, during, and after the performance to ensure that you get that response?

Remember the Swiffer? Swiffer positions itself as a product that is all benefit: It transforms dusting from a chore into fun. We never hear a lot of details about the product's features, and that undoubtedly allows it to remove any frustration from the dusting process. And yet, these features deliver on the promise of the benefit. The result is tremendous product satisfaction—and a lot of buzz about an ordinary household product.

Brand managers should ask themselves: How do people perceive my brand? How can I consolidate that perception and feed it back into my brand experience? At the same time, how can I validate my consumer for building my reputation? How can I make them feel secure in continuing to maintain it?

The worst-case scenario, of course, is that you somehow let the quality of your product—and the level of customer satisfaction—slip. If that happens, two things occur:

- Customer discontent grows

- The customer who referred you and helped to build your reputation will be embarrassed for referring you in the first place

The result? The value of your word-of-mouth will drop from an asset to a liability.

For the opposite to happen, consistency of approach and messaging is a must. The MGM Grand Hotel and Resort in Las Vegas promises "maximum Vegas." In other words, it tries to gather the best expressions of the Vegas experience under one roof. This can range from high-end French restaurants such as L'Atelier de Joël Robuchon, to a new European-style pool, to the exclusive, high-end accommodations at Skylofts and the ultra-exclusive Mansion (where guests are welcome by invitation only). For customers who listen, the message is consistent throughout the experience. If they are receptive to that message and have been satisfied with their experiences, the message becomes part of how satisfied customers talk about MGM Grand, reinforcing the brand's growing reputation.

Red Bull is seen as a fun, rebellious, outlaw brand. This is part of its appeal and part of what draws new users to the drink. Although it does engage in traditional advertising, Red Bull devotes most of its marketing dollars to staging events that are about fun, self-irony, and rebellion. By doing so, it walks the brand talk and contributes to reputation's positive feedback loop.

As with individual personality, of course, brand personality can be fluid. There are times when the way people talk about you can be a threat to the continued success of your brand. In situations like these, it is important to try and work against that negative talk with constructive gestures.

Think of Wal-Mart. It has always had—and still enjoys— a reputation for low prices. This continues to be an important consumer draw, thanks to a consistent pricing policy. At the same time, however, Wal-Mart earned a negative reputation as a destroyer of communities because it made business diffi- cult for small-town competitors. To work against that negative perception, it has integrated counter-balancing aspects to the experience of shopping there. Famously, when you walk into Wal-Mart, you are greeted personally and made to feel wel- come. More recently, Wal-Mart has agreed to allow people with RVs to set up camp in its parking lots. Cross-country drivers can rest assured that, if there is no room for them at the trailer park, they can count on Wal-Mart to provide a safe landing spot. With the effect of these RVs cropping up in parking lots nationwide, the chain has fostered the creation of a new kind of community.

Both Innocent Drinks and Pret A Manger have leveraged continuity in their favor. Each company promises a revolution in food consumption by offering fresher, tastier fare. However, where other companies might take customer satisfaction with these as cues to rest easy, each delivers on the promise of revo- lution by implementing truly healthy and sustainable practices. Innocent has taken steps to reduce its carbon footprint and packages its product in unique, 100% recycled plastic bottles. Pret A Manger also uses biodegradable packaging and has vowed to remain private (and, if necessary, less profitable) to deliver on its vision.

Like all the other meaning-driven engines of Conversational Capital, the workings of continuity are essentially existential. To make your brand experience one whose reputation is a self-fulfilling engine of positive word-of-mouth, you have to begin by knowing who you are. And then, you have to remain true to who your constituents truly want you to be.

WE LIKE TO WALK AROUND THE OFFICE IN COWBOY BOOTS, TUTUS, AND TOP HATS

You can exert a great deal of control over your image. In writing this book, we tried to make a good impression and back it up with cogent observations. We hope you think highly of us. However, it doesn't take much for a reputation to be compromised, especially when people are free to say whatever they want about you. Conversational Capital suggests that you can exert more control over how people talk about you by ensuring that the experience you deliver is in line with a positive perception of you. So that means no walking around in silly outfits for us.

(By the way, that whole cowboy boots and tutus thing is just a vicious rumor someone started. It's completely untrue. The top hats, maybe, but just on special occasions....)

SUMMING UP

Conversational Capital demands continuity. Because it is about creating consistent brand stories, it works best when there is no disconnect between how a product is designed, marketed, and perceived. The best brands are the result of a united, cohesive strategy, and they walk the talk.

QUESTIONS FOR DISCUSSION

Is there no room for error?

This book cites leaders and category changers who are continuity kings and queens. Nevertheless, in the normal course of business, compromises must be made and quotidian reality wrestled with. Even among the best, there is room for improvement. Often, these leaders are working against systemic inertia. So, yes, everyone is free to make mistakes. Consumers are demanding, but they can also be forgiving when they love you.

PART THREE

IMPLEMENTING CONVERSATIONAL CAPITAL

18.

GETTING STARTED

Why should marketers implement Conversational Capital? Because, as we've demonstrated, *Conversational Capital will drive growth* through a three-step process:

1. Conversational Capital positively augments consumer satisfaction by increasing the resonance of brand experiences.

2. Resonant consumer experiences fuel positive word-of-mouth.

3. Positive word-of-mouth enables you to reduce marketing and promotional costs while driving growth.

It's no longer enough to deliver consumer satisfaction. Indeed, as consumer tastes and expectations become more sophisticated, consumer satisfaction has been relegated to "green fee" status. It's the price of entry for any consumer experience. Without it, marketers are doomed to failure.

Experiences can no longer be just satisfactory—to get talked about, people have to find them meaningful. They can't just like an experience, they have to *love* it.

Sounds great—so how do you do it?

1. ASSEMBLE THE RIGHT TEAM

Implementing Conversational Capital is not a simple process. Rather, it presents a challenge to your organization because it requires significant change. Implementation extends to the roots of who you are and how you work. It is, therefore, important that you assemble a team that is completely dedicated to the task at hand. There can be no shortcuts.

The operative word here is "team." Implementation must be a group effort because diversity of talent and viewpoint, analytical ability, perspective, and debate are required. As you will see, implementing Conversational Capital requires work-shopping and prototyping—ideally, the province of groups and teams. Having a team in place enables talented individuals to bounce great ideas around and improve on them.

If you've worked in such a collaborative manner before, you know that the team must truly be balanced. It can't be controlled by a single, charismatic leader. Because even the most exceptional, talented, and inspiring individuals are limited by a set of personal references. Yes, great leaders have accomplished incredible things—but no one knows *everything*. Often, strong individuals will be driven to confirm what they already believe. They need others who will challenge them, spot their blind spots, and call them on their weaknesses (while, of course, celebrating and learning from their excellence).

On the other end of the scale, the team can't include only technocrats. This is because implementation requires the insight and inspiration strong individuals bring to the table. In our experience, teams should be composed of talented A-listers. These are people at the management level who are self-confident enough to express ideas and dissent. They are talented, cultured individuals capable of composing and driving a high-level vision while maintaining an obsession with minutiae. These people don't accept whatever idea is thrown at them— they revel in the ability to challenge their own thinking and that of others while ultimately asserting the ability to coalesce around a ***disruptive*** idea.

The ultimate goal is to create conditions within which creativity will thrive. Your organization must become a creativity incubator. By assembling a *multidisciplinary* team, you can ensure a diversity of perspective that is essential to creative thinking. Your team should be small enough to function efficiently; we recommend a maximum of four to five members.

When we assemble creative teams at SID LEE, we try to assemble the most wildly diverse talents possible. Team members should have surprising skill sets and compelling stories of their own. We bring together strategists, light designers, set designers, costume designers, industrial designers, architects, writers, retail specialists, and filmmakers. We have even invited DJs and a circus clown onto certain projects, and we have an oceanographer on staff.

Each of these individuals brings a different point of view to the work at hand. Plan a new retail space, and the D.J. will be thinking about the over-all mood and sound first. The architect will consider the tectonics and physical properties of the space. The writer will be pre-occupied with the over-arching narrative. A retail specialist will be concerned first and foremost with revenue per square foot. The clown, who has performed on live stages around the world, knows how to provoke people and get a laugh out of them (though he has yet to wear flap shoes to a meeting).

You might be asking, "Doesn't bringing strong individuals together without a leader invite chaos?" The answer is that a certain form of creative directorship *is* required. Conversational Capital teams demand the leadership of someone we think of as being half suit and half circus ringmaster—someone who can encourage creativity while keeping the tiller straight. This person must be capable of digging out consumer insight, understanding business economics, and leading creative talent. She requires a balance of left- and right-brain skills. Lastly, she needs to be a great listener with an ability to simplify and synthesize both problems and solutions.

2. CARRY OUT A CONVERSATIONAL CAPITAL AUDIT

You might already be a Conversational Capital all-star. Conversely, you might be trying to pull your brand out of a nose dive. Maybe you're neither. You might be liked—but not loved. You might just have started a business. In any case, after you assemble your team, your first task is to establish where you stand in terms of Conversational Capital.

To do this, you must carry out an audit. Audits are about mining internal and external information to build an understanding of where your offering succeeds or fails. This can enable you to identify the points at which your experience falls flat and into which you can inject saliency and resonance.

We begin by asking basic questions about consumer satisfaction, both in your organization and among consumers. These follow:

- Are consumers satisfied with this product or experience?

- Are they compelled to talk about it?

- Would they talk about it if asked?

- Would they talk about it if unsolicited?

While you ask these questions, you need to audit the experience of competing brands and ask the same questions to see if they are telling resonant stories. What are they conveying? What does it mean to customers?

Remember that you are testing your experience for its *residual value*. Essentially, Conversational Capital increases this value by giving you a story to enjoy and employ long after the immediate experience of a product or service is over.

These questions might appear basic, but they can give you a good idea of how much residual value consumers experience, if any. Knowing how much or how little tells you how much more deeply you need to go into your audit. The best news would be to reaffirm that people still love and rave about you all the time. By examining the experience of your competitors, you will at least have uncovered insights into the latest trends and developments, and staked out room for continued improvement. If, on the other hand, you are the subject of consistent negative talk, or if no one is satisfied enough with your experience to discuss it at all, you have to go deeper.

This involves asking a few questions. Remember that, as you examine these questions, you should also ask how your competition answers them for a more accurate analysis. Also, don't forget that they should be directed both internally in your organization and externally with consumers.

- **The *Consumer Path***

  What is the complete arc of a consumer's interaction with your experience? How and why did they choose it? Is it, for instance, positive word-of-mouth—a good sign—or aggressive pricing (not so good) that drive them to you? What steps did they take to get to it? Did they have to overcome hurdles? Was the process seamless? How did they go through the experience itself? What happened after?

- **The Senses**

  How does the experience affect the full range of your senses, both positively and negatively? Do people rave about how stimulating or meaningful it was, or did it leave them flat or worse?

- **The Form, Function, and Flow**

  What does your experience promise? How well does the flow of the experience pay it off? At how many consumer touchpoints is the potential of that promise maximized?

- **The Problem Points**

  Where does the experience break down (if at all)? Is there any point at which it is not continuous and integrated? Are you over-promising and under-delivering? Why is this happening?

- **The Story**

  What story are you trying to tell through your experience? Does it make sense? Is it fresh and inspiring? Is it there at all? *Understanding your story and getting it across is absolutely essential to Conversational Capital*—that's why we go into this process in much more detail in the following section.

- **The *Customers***

  What are your customers getting out of the experience?

  It's not enough that a brand tells a story. In the end, that story must be compelling. Ultimately, you must ask, *"How are consumers benefiting from this experience?"* This begs the most important question of all, in terms of Conversational Capital: Is this experience identity-shaping?

Asking these questions can help you determine the saliency and resonance of your experience. After you have, you are ready to move to the next stage: designing solutions.

DID YOU HEAR THE ONE ABOUT THE CLOWN, THE EXHIBITIONIST, AND THE OCEANOGRAPHER?

We assembled the wildest combinations of people to generate creativity. That's because bringing together as many perspectives as possible can help you see reality in a new light, generate insight, and come up with solutions. You need to be tough with yourself and positive at the same time. Conversational Capital hinges on daring to be different—and to swim in tricky waters without a lifeguard.

Yes, we worked with every one of the characters mentioned. It is fun—if you keep them away from sharp objects!

SUMMING UP

To begin implementing Conversational Capital, you must do the following:

- *Assemble a multidisciplinary team to enhance creativity and encourage insight.*
- *Carry out a Conversational Capital audit by asking these questions:*

  1. *What drives the consumer to interact with your brand experience?*
  2. *How does your experience affect the full range of our senses, both positively and negatively?*
  3. *Where and how do guests interact with your experience?*
  4. *Where does the experience break down, if at all?*
  5. *What story are you trying to tell through your experience?*
  6. *What are consumers getting out of your story? Is it identity-shaping?*

QUESTIONS FOR DISCUSSION

Can I do this work myself?

Yes, at least partly. We never intended this book as a sales pitch for our business. We sincerely believe that simply by following the suggestions and answering the questions in this section, you can end up with a better understanding of how Conversational Capital can help you develop a more compelling brand. Of course, not everyone can bring together a D.J., filmmaker, industrial designer, and professional clown around the same project, but we're not going to stop you from trying. In your opinion, who do you think would make the best players on a Conversational Capital team?

19.

DESIGNING A SOLUTION

Having completed your audit, you can begin to truly assess where you stand. To help you do so, we crafted a questionnaire that helps you distinguish between levels of Conversational Capital, available at www.conversationalcapital.com. The goal is to provide an action plan specific to your strengths and weaknesses. After you use it, you will find that your brand experience fits into one of five possible categories.

Your position on the pyramid is determined by a combination of two factors: client satisfaction and salience. At the top of the pyramid, you are rich in both. As you descend, the amount of both decreases:

1. The Sweet Spot: You are rich in Conversational Capital. People love you and have made you part of their lifestyle.

2. Advocacy: People speak well of you. Congratulations!

3. Passive Endorsement: Customers are satisfied but not vocal.

4. Silence: No one talks about you.

5. Negative Word-of-Mouth: Houston, we've got trouble.

The pyramid is a critical tool because it enables you to understand where you stand in terms of Conversational Capital. If you are in the Sweet Spot, you excel at Conversational Capital. Just below that, your clients are highly satisfied, but you could use the eight engines of Conversational Capital to amplify your experience and move your consumers to the top. Things get a little more problematic in the middle. Here, people are more or less satisfied, but your experience is not salient. More work is needed.

If you are in the bottom two tiers, this book might not be for you. Your main problem is one of consumer satisfaction. We could apply as much Conversational Capital as we can to your brand, but your problem is more fundamental at the management and operations level. We could tell the most compelling story about you that we could imagine, but if your staff treats your customers with contempt and your product is deadpan, it just wouldn't work. It's inescapable: The lower you are when you begin, the more wrenching the necessary change will be.

GENERATING INSIGHT

Knowing where you stand, you can move to the next stage: generating insight. Your team is in place, the data is at hand, and now it's time to work. This is where we run into a rough patch.

We have not seen a great book on insight, and this is not going to be it. For all the business cases in the world a professor offered an easy solution to, no one can tell you how that solution was arrived at. The best we can do is tell you what ingredients are necessary to make the magic happen. Then, we can tell you how to optimize the use of whatever insight you arrive at.

To begin, it is important to define what insight is—and even that isn't easy. Insight is a penetrating vision into the heart of things. It reaches beneath the surface and outside of conventional boundaries to grasp the essence of what must be done. It isn't advertising's "Big Idea." Rather, it is that "aha!" moment when you can state, simply and succinctly, what a brand needs. It fuels the implementation of Conversational Capital, the bedrock on which you base your creative efforts. Without insight, it is impossible to move forward. It impacts and guides the entire creative development that we attempt to describe in the next pages.

Where does it come from? In our experience, it comes from examining three things:

1. **Your brand's D.N.A.** What is this brand supposed to be about? Where is it going? Why?

2. **Consumer needs.** What are your consumers looking for? What do they want?

3. **Reinvention.** How could your brand be reworked and optimized in the best way possible?

If you juggle these long enough, a truth will emerge, and you will recognize it. That is insight.

When you recognize it, you notice that insight is a combination of the following:

- Creative thinking and analysis

- Intensity

- Intuition

- Knowledge

- Data

- Imagination

Remember that insight, when won, is precious. People often lose sight of their insight or don't make the most of it. Here is what you can do to keep it at the forefront of your thinking and maximize its potential:

- State the insight in a sentence (10 words or less).

- Answer the five Ws: *What* are we trying to achieve? *Who* is this intended for? *Why* are we doing this? *Where* is the best place to make this happen? *When?*

- Ensure consistency in the tone, manner, and behavior of your brand.

- Finally, after you do all these things, figure out the *how.*

EXERCISE CREATIVITY

If generating insight is tricky, where does that leave creativity? The essential nature of creativity is that it defies formulas and easy categorization. So, rather than over-simplify or make empty promises, we suggest the following exercises, which might help you come up with creative solutions. Of course, before you read them, we remind you that putting together multidisciplinary teams to go over them will be invaluable.

1. GET YOUR STORY STRAIGHT

Your story is the atomic center of Conversational Capital. Each of the examples we cite throughout this book is informed by a central narrative: what we call the **meta-story**. The Apple experience tells a story about innovation, individuality, and freedom (nothing much has changed since the 1984 commercial). Cirque du Soleil tells a story about human potential, youth, excitement, and optimism. The adidas story is about technical excellence, the triumph of the human spirit, and international unity.

In this respect, leading brands are like outstanding individuals: They *own* their story like no one else. It is what sets them apart and draws people to them.

Determining your story is where we start. Sometimes, it can be evident at first glance. Your story might be obvious to outsiders, even if it isn't to you (isn't that often the case with people, too?).

As playwrights, novelists, and screenwriters may tell you, sometimes the story is right there, trying to get through—all you have to do is get out of its way. We discussed the case of Virgin earlier. Because it gathers a staggering amount of loosely associated brands under one banner, it's hard to remember what the Virgin story is. Richard Branson will say that they are all Virgin companies because they reflect his personal interests. But is that enough? Despite what he says, Richard's Branson meta-story keeps pushing its way through, and it's inspiring. At heart, Branson is a risk-taking explorer. That's a deep well to draw from—could Virgin itself be reconfigured to consistently deliver a sense of risk taking and exploration?

It is helpful to think of your meta-story as the over-arching notion that makes your experience meaningful and sets it apart.

The degree to which you have to dig to find your story depends on where you stand in terms of consumer satisfaction and experience saliency. The engines of Conversational Capital are there to help you get through the process.

2. USE THE ENGINES OF CONVERSATIONAL CAPITAL AS YOUR GUIDE

Examine an experience for the presence of the engines of Conversational Capital, and they become signposts that lead you back to your core story.

For example, your experience might contain a founding myth (like Richard Branson's Virgin). What does it tell you about your experience today? Is your founding myth still relevant? If so, is that relevance clear to your customers? If you strayed from it, would it be useful to come back to it again? Could you benefit from a back-to-basics approach?

Some aspect of your experience might be iconic: a logo, building, or sculpture. What does it tell us about you? Is there something in Virgin's iconic logo that can become a beacon of centralized meaning for the now too diffuse brand?

The same is true for RSO and EPO. Is there any way in which your experience stands out that tells us something meaningful about you? Do you over-deliver in one aspect of your experience or another? How can this be leveraged in your favor?

Tribalism might be the individual engine of Conversational Capital that reveals most about your experience—because it tells us who your story is meant to appeal to. If we are told a story is for sensitive children or weepy-eyed romantics or world-weary cynics, we know a lot about it before the telling even begins. Story and tribe are intrinsically connected. This is more than a mere matter of targeting—which takes into account surface variables, such as age and income—because it challenges us to consider how tribe and experience are to be connected at the deepest, most meaningful level.

3. MULTIPLY YOUR CULTURAL REFERENCES

In assembling our teams, we also try to multiply our cultural references as much as possible. Why? By multiplying cultural references, individuals in a multidisciplinary group adopt an even more supple and flexible sense of perspective, further enhancing the ability to be creative.

This might come naturally to us, living in Montréal. We're bilingual—thinking and speaking in French and English every day enables one to develop a flexible, bifocal view of the world. This thing you sit on isn't just a "chair," for example, it's a "*chaise*." What makes the words different? How are they the same? What does looking at the phenomenon of a chair from the perspective of two languages at once tell you about the essential, metalingual "chairness" of a chair?

We're also Canadian—which means we're kind of American and kind of European, but at heart, neither. So our perspective on both cultures, sitting on the fringe, enables us to see what people living inside them sometimes don't.

You don't have to speak two languages or be Canadian, of course. But an individual's background in design, or architecture, or filmmaking, or English literature, or art history can shape his perspective in different ways. Put those individuals into a group and the result can be alchemical. Make those individuals from different countries, or age groups, or interest communities, and the results can be explosive.

Multiplying cultural references also makes you more competitive. If you expand your focus from what's happening right around you to what's happening everywhere, you get a much clearer picture of where the bar is truly being set. Knowing what the best are doing around the world challenges you to be even better.

4. ASK YOURSELF WHERE YOU CAN CREATE THE MOST MARKET DISCONTINUITY

As we've seen, Conversational Capital is often about standing out from the crowd. Perhaps you can conceive of a market gap that your experience could fill. When creating a new experience, it's good to ask how you could stand out from the crowd (the same is true if you're reinvigorating and refreshing an existing one). Find out where you have space to stand out and then widen that space. This can translate into a competitive advantage. Conversational Capital happens if you zig when everybody else zags.

5. CHALLENGE THE STATUS QUO

Marketers driven by an ambitious personal vision always challenge the status quo. Before Bill Gates, Steve Jobs, Richard Branson, and Guy Laliberté, there was nobody quite like them. Each had a vision that redefined their market. If you are such an entrepreneur or if you work for an organization that is driven by an ambitious entrepreneurial vision, you don't have to search far to see how and where you stand out. What makes you different should be the basis of your story.

6. MANIPULATE TIME

Step outside of the reality you live in and make up your own. If you had to build a breakthrough brand tomorrow, and you could do whatever you wanted, what would you do? Look at the results of your thinking and apply them to the work at hand.

7. RIDE THE ENGINES OF CONVERSATIONAL CAPITAL LIKE A TEAM OF HORSES FROM HELL

Milk the engines of Conversational Capital for all they are worth. Make sure your story is getting out to the market by seeing where you can leverage Icons, EPO, Endorsement, Myth, RSO, Continuity, and Tribalism. Drill down through one at a time and don't stop until you run out of ideas.

8. BORROW FROM OTHER CATEGORIES

Take at look at the best practices in other industries and ask yourself what you can learn from them. If you run a restaurant, can you learn anything from a high-end spa? If you're in the book-selling business, can you learn anything from how music and film are sold?

9. SPOT THE UNFULFILLED NEED

Take a close look at your market and ask yourself if there is a need that is not being catered to. Sometimes, filling such a market gap creates sufficient opportunity for you to tell a compelling story. Many of the successes we have pointed to time and again happened because someone set out to answer a need that no one else was fulfilling. Cirque du Soleil instinctively filled a market need for more sophisticated circus entertainment. The MINI Cooper filled a need for a certain kind of small car. Before Cracker Jack came along, who thought the world needed a box of caramelized popcorn with a prize in it?

Note that in each of these three cases, a type of over-delivery was at work. No one was actively demanding any of these things. Instead, the need was unstated; it was out there "in the air." The creative entrepreneurs behind these successful ventures sensed the need before anyone could express it.

Whatever category you're in, you should ask yourself if there could possibly be a gap that someone else hasn't filled. For instance, why has no one created a premium discount airline? Why isn't there a chain of family restaurants that sells gourmet health food? Why isn't there a high-end hotel experience where security is given the same importance as luxury?

If it makes intuitive sense to you, and if consumer research further demonstrates that you could fill a potential need, you should definitely explore the possibility. After all, the thought that drives creative thinking isn't "me too." It is: "I wonder if this would work?"

10. WHEN IN DOUBT, IMPROVISE

If, after going through all of these, you're still stuck, why not try a few improvisational exercises? The first rule of Improv is "yes, and...." It's learning how to be open, flexible, and accepting, and then working with that. It's also about breaking down categories and seeing things in a new light.

Sites like www.improvencyclopedia.org show you up to 500 improv exercises that help to build team spirit and encourage fresh thinking. You may feel silly doing them, but if you're in a rut, they'll help. Remember: When you're brainstorming, there are no wrong answers. You are not being judged!

STARTING TOMORROW, EVERYONE IN YOUR OFFICE MUST COME TO WORK WEARING YELLOW JUMPSUITS AND FLOWER POTS ON THEIR HEADS

Come on, you know we're kidding. However, implementing Conversational Capital might require change as significant as making your staff dress like Devo. You have to consider putting together teams in a new way and challenging how you see yourselves and the world. You must be ready to ask some fundamental questions about how you operate—and then be ready to change.

Of course, you probably can do it all without changing your Casual Friday policy.

SUMMING UP

In designing Conversational Capital solutions, two things are absolutely necessary: insight and creativity.

Despite what some people might promise, there is no recipe for either. We offer some guidelines, however:

- *Know yourself and your story.*
- *Know what people want.*
- *Assemble a multidisciplinary team.*
- *Multiply your cultural references.*
- *Dare to be different.*
- *Think like an entrepreneur.*
- *Use the engines of Conversational Capital.*

QUESTIONS FOR DISCUSSION

Can anyone be creative?

The truth is, we believe that some people are, by their nature, more creative than others. Similarly, some people are just more insightful than others. There is a strange kind of alchemy at work. However, we also sincerely believe our recommendations can maximize your analytical and creative potential, wherever you're starting from in terms of natural ability.

Do you think we're way off the mark? Let us know what happens if you follow our advice.

20.

IMPLEMENTATION

Building from insight, you have arrived at a creative solution. Now you can begin implementing. The implementation of Conversational Capital is a dance of many steps, and it goes like this:

1. **Package** your ideas.

2. **Build** a *prototype*.

3. **Monitor** your progress.

4. **Roll Out** your experience.

5. **Improve** your work.

The following sections describe what happens at each stage.

PACKAGING

Packaging your idea means giving it flesh—putting it into a physical form that makes it easy for everyone to understand. It involves taking your idea out of the abstract, ineffable world of thought and expressing it in such a way that even the least sophisticated can grasp and get behind it.

That physical form can be anything. It can range from a script and layout to a video or to a complete architectural model. Simply put, you must choose the form that best conveys what you are trying to get across. However complex your idea, it should be a simple, comprehensive expression of what you want to achieve, graspable by both the left and right brain. A single glance at it should give you an excellent idea of the final form. A more penetrating look should reveal its subtler details.

The purpose of packaging is three-fold.

On one level, it enables you to examine your work with a new perspective. When you have packaged a project, you take advantage of the opportunity it presents to see if you have used the Eight Engines of Conversational Capital to their fullest potential. Ask the difficult questions. Have you got a compelling story that stands together? Have you injected as much myth as you can? Ritual? EPO? RSO? Tribalism? Endorsement? Icons? Is the experience continuous?

Remember, Conversational Capital is about stimulating the senses in a resonant manner. Therefore, you must package your idea in such a way that it leverages as much sensual interaction as possible. How is your project going to sound, feel, taste, look, and smell? Can your package convey this?

Up until now, you've worked selectively with your hand-picked team of A-listers. Executing your idea requires the efforts of an expanded team. The bridge between an insightful idea and a reality that generates conversation is a proper brief that enables everyone on your team to understand what they have actualized and why.

In the world of advertising and communications, the brief has become an art-form. We'd like to take some of the mystery and intimidation out of writing a strong brief. The following are our observations. A brief is a succinct (no more than one page) outline of what is to be done. You should:

- State the big idea in no more than one sentence.

- Express the story to be told.

- Mention how and why that story matters to consumers.

- Answer the five Ws: who, what, where, when, and why.

- Include relevant benchmarks if they exist.

- Ensure that your brief is stated simply enough that it can be understood by just about anyone.

- Be comprehensible to a 7 year old (we kid you not).

If you do your job properly, your intentions and purpose will be clear to everyone. A clear, properly presented brief facilitates stakeholder buy-in.

After buy-in has occurred, you can rest assured that all players are ready for the next stage: prototyping.

After buy-in has occurred, and you are assured that all players are ready for the next phase, the package comes to its ultimate use. It enables an excellent brief. With the proper brief, you are ready for the next stage: prototyping.

PROTOTYPING

You begin the prototyping phase by briefing everyone who needs to carry the project forward. Your brief enables writers, industrial designers, architects, marketers, public relations persons, and anyone else involved in the project to share an understanding and speak the same language. It provides a supreme level of cohesion.

The result is to arrive at a working prototype of your experience. Naturally, this differs depending on the nature of the project at hand. The point is to get it as close to final reality as possible, so that you proceed to the next stage: monitoring.

An important component of the prototyping stage is what we call Running the Economic Reality test. This is a necessary step; it is the point at which traditional project management takes on increased importance. After you have given creativity open reign and documented the results in detail, you have to consider what is economically feasible. Some ideas may just be too expensive (for now). Other ideas may be so good that it makes sense to invest a little more than you planned.

MONITORING

You may have noted that, up until this point, Conversational Capital has not relied on traditional forms of consumer interaction like focus groups or testing. Nevertheless, consumer interaction is essential, and this is where it comes in.

After you have arrived at a working prototype, you must allow consumers to use it and provide feedback. It is crucial that the prototype be made accessible in conditions that are as close to its real-world application as possible. Conversational Capital is not measured well in laboratory conditions. One has to take into account the real-world context your project will exist in.

Monitoring will enable you to see how well you have done in terms of saliency and satisfaction. If you are falling short in any area, it provides you an opportunity to repair and adjust using the eight engines as your guide and measuring stick. If you generate an excellent reaction, you can use the monitoring process to see if there are areas in which you can perform even better.

After you have made these adjustments, you are ready to roll out.

ROLLING OUT

Rolling your experience out to the market isn't simply a matter of putting it where consumers can get at it. Instead, it requires a large amount of internal organization first.

Just as all important players must be united around a common brief during prototyping, so too does everyone in your organization need to be gathered around a common purpose at roll out. Your experience may contain the greatest Conversational Capital known to history, but if there are people in the organization who don't get and can't communicate it to your clients, it won't work.

Roll out must include extensive employee education and training. Each person must know the story you are telling, and what his role is in getting it across. Those who interact regularly with your clients, such as retail staff and customer service representatives, must know how Conversational Capital impacts on customer care, and critically, how they can actualize it.

Once and only once this job is done can you bring your project to market. Luckily, the engines of Conversational Capital serve as a handy guide to your story and purpose.

IMPROVEMENT

Implementation doesn't end at rollout. We firmly believe that bringing your project to market is only the first step. What follows is a continual process of adjustment and improvement. It is something the brands we admire have been doing for years.

When Cirque du Soleil premieres a new show, it is never quite finished. In the tradition of theatrical "work shopping," paying audiences are invited to view a work-in-progress. The show's creators then adjust the show based on audience reaction. What bored them? What got the biggest laugh? The most audible thrill? Based on the answer to these questions, they think about how the show could be tightened up. Live acts do it all the time. It's not a question of pandering. Rather, the show creators understand that they are in dialogue with the audience.

Even after the initial fine-tuning of a show, Cirque du Soleil's artistic directors and cast continue to work on it as new audiences in new cities react in their own ways to the material. It keeps the Cirque experience fresh and interesting. Watch a show in Montréal, and you'll see one thing. See it a year later in Seattle, and you'll experience something else.

What does this teach us about Conversational Capital? Simply that the best experiences are living, evolving phenomena, and that it is essential to listen to what consumers are telling you. Consumer reactions tell you where your story could use more work, be made fresher and more relevant. They can tell you, specifically, which engines of Conversational Capital are working for you and which need work.

This process works efficiently if you employ at the earliest phase possible beta testing. In essence, this is what Cirque is doing with its audiences early on a tour. It works because it creates an opportunity for consumers to feel like *prosumers* (consumers who have an influence on production). Early Cirque du Soleil adopters are aware that they are privileged participants in work-shopping sessions. Apple resorts to loyal beta testers when planning to unveil new products. Jones Soda's new flavors aren't just sampled by users; they are developed in partnership with them. adidas products are developed for and with top-performing athletes whose feedback becomes an essential part of the company's consumer offering.

As helpful as beta testing can be, however, it is only part of what should be an ongoing habit of listening to what consumers have to say.

If you think about it, this kind of continuous tweaking is something successful retailers have always done instinctively. A successful fashion retailer, for example, will always give itself room to adjust the offering in the face of consumer response. The faster it responds, the more profitable it is likely to be.

Some might see this kind of flexibility as too risky or difficult to manage.

If so, we remind you of the formula that opened this section. Conversational Capital increases experience saliency and turns highly satisfied consumers into experience advocates. This, in turn, drives growth while lowering marketing expenditures.

In an era where change has become inevitable, Conversational Capital can have a transformative effect on your business and give you the power to manage that change in your favor. Isn't that worth the risk?

WE ARE SPENT!

That's it. We've said our piece and revealed all we know about Conversational Capital. Hopefully, you found the read worthwhile. As for us, we're ready for that advertising guy's vacation. Did we ever tell you about this lake in Switzerland we once took a walk around? Say, how come you talk about a place like that and not...?

SUMMING UP

- *The final stage of implementing Conversational Capital involves taking the following steps:*

  1. *Package your idea.*
  2. *Prototype your project.*
  3. *Monitor the feedback it generates.*
  4. *Roll your project out to market.*
  5. *Improve that product by taking into account consumer feedback.*

- *Before you roll out your product, you must maximize sensory impact to unite players around a common brief and vision. At key moments, you must listen closely to consumer feedback in terms of saliency and satisfaction to see how you can take Conversational Capital to even higher levels.*

QUESTIONS FOR DISCUSSION

Is that all we have to say?

No way. As we have said throughout this book, we hope this discussion continues at www.conversationalcapital. com and that you feel free to participate. In the next chapter, we will also address a few more questions to close off the book and finish with a final thought. Thanks for reading!

21.

AND TWO MORE QUESTIONS

DOES CONVERSATIONAL CAPITAL MAKE ECONOMIC SENSE?

Nothing displeases number crunchers more than unpredictability, except maybe waste. Conversational Capital is based on unquantifiable factors, such as creativity and insight. It is built on story rather than flow charts. How economically sound can it be?

We suggest that it makes much more economic sense to invest in Conversational Capital than in traditional marketing. The efficacy of traditional marketing—especially mass-media advertising—has always been notoriously difficult to track. One can measure awareness levels as an indicator of a campaign's success, but it has always been trickier to establish causality between awareness and sales. Direct marketing and the Web provide a clearer view, because, in these media formats, one can more accurately measure response. Despite this, however, it is a running industry gag that as much as 50 percent of every advertising dollar is lost to the advertiser.

We consider 50 percent to be unacceptably high. If that much revenue is wasted, we propose that companies reapportion it to create Conversational Capital. This can positively impact the bottom line by aligning your walk with your talk. Your product designers can then be empowered to vest your experience with meaning, something customers crave.

By contrast, traditional marketing simply tells consumers they will experience something special. It does nothing to deliver on the promise. Conversational Capital delivers, not just by directly impacting the end experience, but also by *making the communications process an integral and continuous part of that experience.*

Conversational Capital brings new life to Marshall McLuhan's proposition that "the medium is the message." When you save an Apple ad onto your iPod, where does the medium end and where does the message begin? Where does it end or begin when a brand ambassador for any experience enthusiastically shares it with others?

One thing is certain: Positive word-of-mouth results in timely, measurable results. Implement Conversational Capital, and you'll know soon if it worked or not because the Excel spreadsheets don't lie.

DOES CONVERSATIONAL CAPITAL APPLY TO CONSUMER EXPERIENCES ALONE?

When we first began working on this book, we were convinced we had a "theory of everything." We felt that we were formulating a series of observations that could be applied across a complete range of human activities, including politics, non-profit organizations, and even personal development and interpersonal relationships.

Now that we've come this far, we still believe it. As we've said, Conversational Capital happens when you leverage compelling stories to create meaningful, memorable experiences. The same process applies outside of consumer experience, too.

We believe that the time is ripe for Conversational Capital because it provides a bulwark against creeping standardization. Standardization has created a deflavorized world. We may drive on highways, but we are not encouraged to look at them. If we work in office cubicles, we are literally shut off from a world of sense. We turn a blind eye to the ugly utility poles that run above our sidewalks. Some urban planners argue that we have deliberately removed odors from our environments to "smooth out" our sensory experiences.

That process of shutting out has spread across human experience. We feel that politicians are all the same, so we shut them out. We complain that too many have their hands out, so we shut them out, too. Go to a cocktail party, and you may find a great many people talking about the same things in the same way, and they stare into their ice cubes.

Conversational Capital tells us that we don't have to live this way. It tells us that we can involve and excite our minds, hearts, and senses to create more meaningful experiences. Clearly, some industries, such as the restaurant and hotel industry, are ahead of others in understanding this. Conversational Capital can have a transformative effect on the other industries as well.

What if a real estate development included an iconic tower sporting solar panels to power street lights? What if that development collected water for recycling to feed a communal garden where grapes were cultivated for a truly local wine? What if a retail space contained dressing rooms large enough for three people with mirrors that included interactive screens so users could see themselves in different environments? What if some part of that retail space was a working studio where bands rehearsed or street artists created murals? What if an airport waiting lounge was scented with lavender and contained massage tables and bowls of fresh fruit? What if the jetbridge contained a sound installation by a progressive music collective?

These areas and others are currently largely unexplored. However, we have implemented some of these ideas for various clients. As we said, we think it's tremendously exciting to make experiences more meaningful and more likely to be talked about, cutting through the clutter. We can make the world more beautiful, more memorable, more compelling, and more fun.

Conversational Capital makes that happen. People will talk, and they should be talking about you.

Let the conversation begin.

GLOSSARY OF TERMS

The following terms appear throughout the book—they appear in bold italic upon first use in the book. The Glossary terms are also discussed more extensively in the Blog on www.conversationalcapital.com.

advocacy—Unheralded and overwhelmingly favorable endorsement.

awareness—The presence of one's knowledge of the existence of a particular brand experience.

bombastic—You know what we're talking about: seemingly high-flown experiences that ring hollow. *Authors' Note:* Our editor gave us lots of grief about this supposed Canadianism, but we couldn't let it go; hopefully that demonstrates our continuity.

brand—A mark of identity, whether it be for a person, place, physical property, organization, or idea.

brand promise—The essential and singular value proposition that a brand projects.

buzz—Hollow, short-lived conversation around a brand. This phenomenon is distinct from *Conversational Capital* because it often originates not from some trait intrinsic to the brand experience itself, but through a stunt perpetrated around it.

consumer path—Maps the process a consumer went through before, during, and after an encounter with a brand. A consumer's path is important because it can yield critical insights into the challenges and opportunities inherent in fostering Conversational Capital.

continuity—Consistency between what you promise, what people expect, and what you deliver.

conversation—When we exchange ideas or thoughts with others, we are engaging in conversation. The premise of Conversational Capital is that these exchanges are valuable for the people, places, property, and indeed, brands that are mentioned within them.

cultural references—Ideas and content drawn from across global culture.

discontinuity—A major shift in an experience that isn't consistent with its competitive set and/or its natural evolution.

disruptive—The power of an experience to stop consumers in their tracks. This isn't about *interruption*, but instead, about leveraging the power of surprise.

Endorsement—Endorsement is not necessarily a matter of celebrities speaking up for you, but rather is a matter for consumers speaking on your behalf in a free and unsolicited manner.

engine—An engine (of Conversational Capital) charges a brand experience with the necessary antecedents to word-of-mouth. The presence of one or more engines of Conversational Capital significantly enhances the likelihood that a brand will be the recipient of favorable conversation.

Exclusive Product Offering (EPO)—Marks the ability to experience something unique and customized—something that is the outgrowth of one's identity.

exclusivity—The opportunity to own something unique.

experience—Is what happens before, during, and after we encounter a brand, person, place, or object. It is the sum of the means by which our emotions and senses have been touched.

Experiential Marketing—Staged experiences that create opportunity for interaction between consumer and producer.

Founding Myth—The story behind the creation of a brand.

green fee—Constitutes the minimum amount of effort and investment necessary to compete in a particular space.

heuristic—A convenient decision-making shortcut.

Icons—Icons present themselves as extremely efficient heuristics; they are signs and symbols rich in evocative power and association.

identity-shaping—The power of a brand experience not merely to mark one's identity, but to transform it. This implies that a particular resonant experience has the power to *change* our identity.

influencers—The people whose opinions and recommendations we value.

Initiation—A subset of ritual, initiation describes a passage from a passive state of involvement to one that is deeper and more meaningful.

insight—A penetrating understanding of what drives consumers and triggers consumption experiences.

intensity—Intense brands are those that engineer experiences that connect with people—that reach, touch, and engage the values and attitudes of a particular audience.

mass-marketing—Promoting goods and services using a simple, easy-to-remember message propagated with heavy repetition through mass media channels.

meta-story—The consumer's over-riding story; it is composed of a number of individual *narratives*.

multidisciplinary—Key to fostering Conversational Capital is the act of assembling *multidisciplinary teams*. An effective team is assembled of talented A-listers who are *not* homogenous; who come from diverse educational, cultural, occupational, and socio-economic realms.

Myths—Foundation stories that shape and inform our culture; they inform who we are, where we came from, and what we aspire to.

narrative—A consumer story or a story of a consumption experience. The aggregate of a consumer's narratives amounts to his or her *meta-story*.

Over-Delivery—A subset of EPO, Over-Delivery defines an aspect of an experience that transcends expectations or industry norms, marking it as singular in its own domain.

personalization—Personalization is about the opportunity to take something generic and imbue it with attributes that are emblematic of *an individual's* values, beliefs, and personality. Personalization is contrasted to EPO (Exclusive Product Offering) because it merely affects surface attributes rather than allowing for fundamental changes in the meaning and substance of an experience.

positioning—The place a brand occupies in a consumer's mind.

poutine—A uniquely Quebecois indulgence composed of french fries, cheese curds, and gravy.

prosumer—Truly intense initiates of a given product or service. They are typically quasi-experts in navigating a chosen consumption experience, and will at times contribute directly to the formulation and design of that experience.

prototype—We craft prototypes to immerse people in complete brand experiences. Typically, prototypes are utilized not simply to test the concept itself, but also to create internal buy-in.

Relevant Sensory Oddity (RSO)—Exhibited when our senses are stimulated and challenged in a way that's intelligent and salient to the consumer's experience.

residual value—The added value consumers enjoy after an experience realized in the form of the stories they tell about it.

resonance—The idea that encounters with brands can trigger a response. Some encounters ring hollow. Resonant experiences seem to touch us in meaningful and palpable ways.

Rituals—Formalized activities which designate that an experience or event is deep in meaning.

saliency / salience—A combination of impact, intensity, and meaning. Simply put, saliency implies that an experience carries meaning and significance in the lives of those who encounter it. The difference between a salient experience and one that lacks salience is that only salient experiences become part of a consumer's story.

satisfaction—The minimal act of meeting customer expectations.

smoked meat—A Montreal delicacy originally conceived by Ashkenazi Rumanian immigrants. Sometimes compared to pastrami, smoked meat is a completely different animal. Best served hot, sandwiched between two slices of rye with a slathering of mustard.

social currency—Content for conversations that helps you shape your identity in the eyes of other people.

standardization—Often credited to Henry Ford, standardization was the product of the mass-marketing age and the industrial revolution. In essence, standardization means that every consumer receives the same product and encounters a *uniform* consumption experience.

story—An experience we share.

touchpoints—Experiences, by their very nature are teaming with opportunities to reach, touch, and engage consumers. These opportunities for contact and stimulation are termed "touchpoints."

Tribalism—Takes place when consumer experiences draw like-minded individuals together in a process of mutual discovery.

tribe—Unlike anthropological tribes which historically banded together based on blood, ethnic ties, or the need for survival, modern tribes are assembled of people united by common interests or consumption behaviors.

whitespace—Fertile yet unoccupied market space. When we create discontinuous brand experiences, we're attempting to own a patch of market whitespace.

word-of-mouth—Consists of the conversations that emerge from our experiences. Often mistermed in discussions about brands as a synonym for endorsement, word-of-mouth instead describes the mere presence of conversations about a particular brand, whether positive or negative.

INDEX

FINANCIAL TIMES

In an increasingly competitive world, it is quality
of thinking that gives an edge—an idea that opens new
doors, a technique that solves a problem, or an insight
that simply helps make sense of it all.

We work with leading authors in the various arenas
of business and finance to bring cutting-edge thinking
and best-learning practices to a global market.

It is our goal to create world-class print publications
and electronic products that give readers
knowledge and understanding that can then be
applied, whether studying or at work.

To find out more about our business
products, you can visit us at www.ftpress.com.